The New York Times

COMPLETE
GUIDE TO THE
NEW TAX LAW

GARY L. KLOTT

Times BOOKS

Library of Congress Cataloging-in-Publication Data

Klott, Gary L., 1949–

The New York Times complete guide to the new tax law.

1. Income tax—Law and legislation—United States.

I. New York Times. II. Title.

KF6369.K58   1986   343.7305′2   86-14441

ISBN 0-8129-1638-7   347.30352

Manufactured in the United States of America

9 8 7 6 5 4 3 2

ACKNOWLEDGMENTS

I owe thanks to many people at *The New York Times* for their help, wisdom and encouragement during my two years covering the tax reform debate on Capitol Hill. My thanks to John M. Lee, assistant managing editor, for bringing me to the *Times* and for his treasured guidance, and to Frederick Andrews, the business editor, for his tutelage, faith, and support.

My special thanks go to Bill Kovach, the Washington bureau chief, and Howell Raines, the deputy, for their tremendous support and guidance during my long stays in Washington, and then for providing a permanent home for me in the Washington bureau for the next tax debate. To Claudia Payne, assistant editor for economics, for her valued counsel. And my thanks to the rest of the editors, reporters, and clerks at the bureau, who made a visitor always feel at home, including David E. Rosenbaum, my colleague on the tax beat, and Jonathan Fuerbringer, who led me through the political maze during the 1984 tax act debate.

I am especially grateful to dozens of tax practitioners and tax economists, many of whom are quoted by name in this book, for their expertise and cherished insights. My special thanks go to Randall Weiss, deputy chief of staff of the Congressional Joint Committee on Taxation, for reading the entire manuscript in its near final form, and to those who read large portions of the manuscript, including Andrew Zuckerman of Arthur Andersen; Michael Wessel, chief tax aide to Representative Richard A. Gephardt; Richard J. Stricof of Seidman & Seidman; and New York tax attorneys Robert A. Spielman and Herbert Paul.

To Jonathan Segal, editorial director of Times Books, for his suggestions, encouragement, and friendship, and to Sarah Trotta, his assistant, for her valued help.

To my brothers, David and Richard, both tax lawyers, for their inspiration and astute insights. And finally to my parents, who have always been a fountain of wisdom and encouragement.

CONTENTS

1

THE NEW TAX LAW: AN OVERVIEW

An Introduction to the New Tax System

The Tax Reform Act of 1986, the most sweeping tax change in the seventy-three-year history of the federal income tax, will touch the lives of every American and business in a fundamental way. From cradle to grave, the new law will affect virtually every aspect of people's financial lives, at home and at the office, and in their dealings with their banker, broker, landlord, and employer. The impact will be felt not only on April 15 but in everyday financial affairs.

Most individuals will see their tax bills reduced by a few hundred dollars a year. But the impact of the new law stretches far beyond the average 6-percent tax cut that individuals are expected to receive.

The new law will affect how people spend, save, borrow, and invest their money. It will shape the way people save for retirement and their children's college education, how much of a pension they will receive from their employer, how much rent they will pay their landlord, what size house they can afford to buy, and the cost of financing everything from cars to vacations.

The new law will have a profound impact in the workplace. The extensive changes Congress made in the corporate income tax promise to reorder the financial fortunes of a large segment of corporate America, affecting where resources flow and where jobs are created and lost.

When Congress passed the Tax Reform Act of 1986 and President Reagan signed it into law on October 22, 1986, the federal government set into motion a radical restructuring of the income tax system that will sharply lower tax rates and curtail dozens of deductions, credits, exclusions, and other special tax breaks that have long been part of the tax code.

1

THE NEW SYSTEM

The new system reduces the top tax rate from 50 percent to 28 percent, the lowest level in more than fifty years. It also condenses the old fifteen-bracket system into just two rate brackets of 15 percent and 28 percent. The new law nearly doubles the size of the personal exemption and also sharply increases the standard deduction, a move that will significantly decrease the number of taxpayers who itemize their deductions.

To pay for all this, many popular tax benefits are eliminated or sharply curtailed. Gone are the deduction for state and local sales taxes, the charitable deduction for non-itemizers, the itemized deduction for personal loan and consumer interest, the income-averaging method of calculating tax liability, the two-earner marriage deduction, preferential treatment of capital gains, and the exclusion for the first $100 ($200 on a joint return) of stock dividends.

Many other tax benefits survive but are scaled back. Millions of middle- and upper-income taxpayers who are covered by a company pension plan will no longer be eligible to claim a deduction for contributions to an Individual Retirement Account (IRA). Medical expenses will be deductible only to the extent that they exceed 7.5 percent of adjusted gross income, instead of 5 percent, preventing an estimated nine million taxpayers who used to claim the deduction from qualifying and providing a smaller benefit for the rest. Deductions for moving expenses and most types of employee business expenses will be available only to itemizers. And employee business expenses and "miscellaneous" itemized deductions, such as union dues and investment expenses, will be deductible only to the extent they exceed 2 percent of adjusted gross income.

Expense-account living also gets wounded. Only 80 percent of the cost of wining, dining, and entertaining customers and clients will be deductible. Students on full scholarships will have to pay tax on part of their income. Unemployment compensation will be fully taxable. And children's savings accounts are no longer treated as kindly as they used to be, requiring many parents to make some adjustments in the way they save for their children's future.

EVEN TAX BENEFITS RETAINED ARE WORTH LESS

Many sacred tax benefits were safeguarded, including the deductions for home mortgage interest, charitable contributions for itemizers, state and local income and property taxes, casualty and theft losses, and the deduction for alimony payments. But even here there were direct or indirect changes.

The deduction for mortgage interest was retained for first and second homes, but new restrictions are imposed that may limit the deductions for people who borrow heavily against the appreciated value of their homes in the future.

But even where deductions are retained in full, they are not worth as much as before. The reason: Tax rates are so much lower. If the tax on income is less, deductions to offset that tax are worth less. Consider someone in the top 50-percent tax bracket under the old law who will move into the 28-percent tax bracket under the new law. His deductions, which used to save him 50 cents on the dollar, will now save him only 28 cents in taxes for each dollar of deductions claimed. For the vast majority of taxpayers, who will be in the 15-percent tax bracket, most deductions will save them no more than 15 cents on the dollar in taxes.

TAXES TO PLAY A SMALLER ROLE IN FINANCIAL AFFAIRS

Indeed, the tax system will play a much smaller role in financial decisions. The tax advantages for taking a particular course over another will be sharply diminished because so many special tax benefits will be curtailed, eliminated outright, or reduced in value by the lower tax rates. And taxpayers will find that they can no longer count as much on the federal government to help underwrite such expenses as business trips, home offices, and uninsured medical expenses or casualty losses.

Although most people will end up with more cash in their pockets to do with as they please because of the tax cut, they will lose many of the tax benefits that for decades have helped subsidize and encourage a long list of common expenditures.

Some people may buy less costly homes or forsake a vacation home because home-owner tax benefits will not provide as much of a subsidy under a system of lower tax rates. Similarly, with rents expected to escalate because of the curtailment of real-estate tax breaks for landlords, apartment dwellers may have to set their sights a bit lower unless they are willing to spend more on housing.

Under the new law, people are likely to think twice before incurring expenses that have long been rationalized on the basis of tax benefits.

Schoolteachers and investors who have relied on the tax code to help finance their vacation travels may end up staying closer to home during hol-

3

idays. Tax deductions for educational travel and trips to investment seminars are abolished by the new law.

Employees who are used to personally footing the bill for work-related expenses may now balk when it comes to buying supplies for the office. In the face of the tough new limits on tax deductions for employee business expenses, many more workers will be demanding reimbursement from their employers.

Some executives may find their companies putting a tighter rein on expense accounts. Between the 20-percent reduction in business meal and entertainment write-offs and the impact of the lower corporate rate on the value of the remaining deduction, companies will find the real cost of a business lunch or a night on the town increases 35 percent under the new law.

And the cost of financing everything from cars to a child's college education will become more expensive, with the deduction for personal interest repealed. Home owners have a way of circumventing the restrictions by borrowing against the home—up to certain limits.

THE INVESTMENT LANDSCAPE ALTERED

The new law will also change the rules of the game and the relative economic merits of the full gamut of investments, from Individual Retirement Accounts to tax shelters. Movie stars, professional athletes, doctors, and other wealthy professionals will discover that investing in railroad boxcars, windmills, shopping centers, and other traditional tax shelters will no longer be useful in whittling their tax bill down to little or nothing.

Real estate, a favorite of investors for generations, will lose some of its luster. Landlords with adjusted gross incomes above $150,000 will no longer be able to write off more expenses than the rental income generated by the property. Indeed, many investors can be expected to shy away from high-risk investments, since the federal government can no longer be counted on to help subsidize losses if a deal turns sour.

Meanwhile, low-risk and high-yield investments, such as bank accounts, money market funds, and bonds and stocks that pay high dividends, are likely to be looked on in a more favorable light than in the past. Their after-tax return will be enhanced by the drop in individual tax rates. But the lower rates will narrow the advantage of tax-exempt municipal bonds over taxable bonds.

4

Investors who own stocks, gold, antiques, and other such assets will find they no longer receive any preferential treatment when they sell their investments. Capital gains will be taxed just like wages.

RETIREMENT ISSUES

The rules governing employer retirement plans are also sharply changed. Millions of workers who change jobs frequently will find the new law provides them with rights to a pension benefit for the first time because of quicker "vesting" requirements. But the new law will also restrict the amount of pay that higher-paid executives can stash away into some tax-deferred company plans, such as the popular "401(k)" employee retirement plans.

REVENUE NEUTRALITY—THE TREASURY GETS
THE SAME AMOUNT

The new tax law was intended to raise the same amount of revenue for the Treasury as the old law—no more, no less. The tax cut for individuals was engineered by shifting more of the tax burden onto corporations. From 1987 through 1991 business will have to pay about $120 billion more, or roughly $24 billion more a year. Individual taxes will be reduced by a similar amount.

A majority of Americans will see their taxes cut, but about one in six will see their tax bills go up. Those with increases are likely to be people who have invested in tax shelters or took substantial advantage of tax benefits that are cut back by the new law.

CORPORATE CHANGES

Although the business community will be bearing a larger share of the tax burden, some industries will fare much better under the new law. The new law curtails a long list of investment incentives and special tax breaks for particular industries. But the law also lowers the corporate tax rate from 46 percent to 34 percent. Thus, retailers, media companies, high-tech firms, service-oriented businesses, and others will benefit handsomely from the drop in the corporate rate, since they never made much use of any special tax breaks or investment incentives. Heavy manufacturers, real-estate developers, large financial institutions, and multinational corporations, however, will suffer from the loss of these special tax breaks.

5

A NEW ERA

The new law ushers in a new era in American economic life. The hundreds of tax changes will lead to sweeping adjustments in the way individuals and corporations do business and arrange their financial affairs.

This book is intended to guide you through the maze of the many significant changes affecting individuals, and some of the major corporate provisions. It offers strategies on how to cope with the new law and save money under it, as well as insights and advice from some of the leading tax authorities in the country.

When the Provisions Take Effect

Most of the provisions of the new tax law are set to take effect on January 1, 1987, when most of the tax benefits are scaled back and tax rates get lowered. But not everything will be fully in place at that point.

Nineteen-hundred-eighty-seven is very much a transition year. Individual and corporate tax rates drop only partway. The top rate for individuals gets lowered to 38.5 percent; for corporations, the top rate drops to 34 percent at midyear. Not until 1988 does the top rate drop to 28 percent for individuals. For most people, the big increase in the standard deduction doesn't come until 1988, and the increase in the personal exemption takes until 1989 to fully phase in.

While most of the tax benefits get cut back immediately in 1987, some are phased out over a period of years to give taxpayers time to adjust. Consumer-interest deductions, for example, will not be entirely eliminated until 1991. In 1987 65 percent of consumer interest will still be deductible, in 1988 40 percent, in 1989 20 percent, and in 1990 10 percent. Tax-shelter losses are generally given the same treatment, though people who invested in tax shelters after the new law was enacted don't get the benefit of the transition.

Many transactions made before the new law was enacted were protected from the tax changes. For example, mortgage debt assumed before August 17, 1986, will be exempt from the new limitations on mortgage-interest deductions. And scholarships and fellowships granted before August 17, 1986, are exempt from the new rules that will make some scholarship payments subject to tax. Many of the retirement provisions also protect previously made contributions to pension plans.

But not all previously made transactions are immune from tax changes. For example, the change in capital-gains rules will apply to previously acquired assets as well as new investments. The phase-out of consumer-interest deductions affects both new loans and old loans. And the harsher tax rules affecting the investment income of children under age fourteen apply to both new and old investments.

The other side of the coin is that income from investments made in years past benefits from the reduced tax rates of the new law, just as will new investments. So interest on a bond that you purchased years ago will now be taxed less harshly under the new law. And a landlord who bought an apartment building years ago will have the rental income taxed at the lower rates.

The first return to incorporate most of the new provisions will be the 1987 return, which is due April 15, 1988.

By and large, the old law still applies for 1986 income tax returns. So the forms you fill out that are due April 15, 1987, will largely be guided by the old law. That includes the right to make a deposit to an Individual Retirement Account and claim a deduction for that deposit on your 1986 return— even if you will not be eligible to claim one under the new law beginning with the 1987 tax year.

Only a few provisions of the new law will be effective earlier than 1987 and incorporated in 1986 tax returns. One is the repeal of the investment tax credit for business equipment and machinery, which was retroactively repealed as of January 1, 1986.

The effective dates for each provision are detailed throughout this book and in the Calendar on page 194.

SPECIALLY TAILORED TRANSITION RULES

Several hundred companies, private organizations, and civic projects were bestowed with different effective dates for certain provisions. Their congressmen were able to obtain for them special "transition rules" that protected some of the tax benefits of the old law for particular projects that had long been in the works. For example, some airlines will still be able to claim investment tax credits on airplanes that they had previously ordered but had not yet placed in service. And a number of planned sports stadiums across the country will be financed without the encumbrance of the new restrictions affecting issuers of tax-exempt bonds.

2

WHY TAX REFORM?

The Decades-Old Battle for Tax Reform

President Reagan launched his campaign to overhaul the federal income tax on January 25, 1984. "Let us go forward with an historic reform for fairness, simplicity and incentives for growth," he said in his State of the Union Address.

But the seeds of the tax reform movement had been sown many years before. President Reagan was not the first president to call for tax reform. Almost every administration since that of President Kennedy had tried to reform the tax system, albeit with little success. Lobbyists for special interests proved too much of a political obstacle. In fact, despite the many attempts at reform, tax breaks continued to proliferate. Since 1967, when tax preferences totaled about $37 billion, they had grown more than tenfold.

As they grew, the philosophical and political underpinnings for an overhaul began to form. The tax reform movement was nourished by such scholars as Joseph A. Pechman, a senior fellow at the Brookings Institution, and Stanley S. Surrey, a Harvard law professor who was an assistant treasury secretary in the late 1960s.

Economists became increasingly concerned that the tax system was distorting investment choices and leading to billions of dollars in misallocated resources. Tax policy experts sensed growing frustration among the general public that the system was becoming ever more complex and unfair, and that the proliferation of special exemptions had led to a higher overall tax burden.

Numerous blueprints for reforming the tax system were introduced by economists and lawmakers. Most of the proposals were similar in framework; tax rates would be sharply reduced by curtailing special tax breaks.

The main differences between the proposals were which tax breaks would be eliminated and how far rates would be lowered.

The one that drew the most attention was a Democratic plan introduced in 1982 by Senator Bill Bradley of New Jersey and Representative Richard A. Gephardt of Missouri, which proposed three rate brackets of 14, 26, and 30 percent for individuals and 30 percent for corporations. The Bradley-Gephardt proposal would serve as one of the guiding doctrines during the tax reform debate.

When President Reagan asked the Treasury Department to come up with a plan to overhaul the tax system, he seized on an issue that had been gaining popularity in the Democratic camp as the 1984 presidential election approached. But the success of tax reform may very well have been due to a convergence of goals of President Reagan and the Democrats. Mr. Reagan's main goal was to reduce tax rates further, while the Democrats wanted to make the system fairer by removing the "loopholes" used by corporations and wealthy individuals.

In Congress, tax reform was near death many times in what was one of the most dramatic legislative sagas in recent history. Some Democrats, while lauding the closing of loopholes, opposed the measure because it did nothing to solve the deficit problem and gave the wealthy a windfall from the sharp drop in tax rates. Many Republicans, while attracted by the lower rates, feared the increased tax burden on business would hurt the economy. Members on both sides of the political aisle also had parochial interests to protect.

The legislation survived because neither party wanted to be blamed for killing it and then be tarnished as being the party of special interests. And even though public opinion polls showed Americans ambivalent about the legislation, many representatives and senators long sensed there was underlying public support for a simpler and fairer system. Furthermore, although a large segment of the business community fought hard to defeat the legislation, congressmen also found some of the leading names of corporate America pushing hard for the legislation because of the lower rates, including companies like General Motors, IBM, Procter & Gamble, Sara Lee, and Beneficial Corporation.

What emerged is the most sweeping overhaul of the tax system since the modern individual income tax was established in 1913. In terms of impact on individuals, the tax law changes during World War II were probably more far-reaching. At that time Congress introduced wage withholding and increased tax rates so that most Americans became subject to income tax for the first time. But in terms of a restructuring of the tax system, the new law is the most sweeping. No other piece of tax legislation—and there have been nearly 60 tax bills since 1913—has changed so many major elements of the tax code in such a fundamental way. The restructuring is so massive that the new law retitles the Internal Revenue Code of 1954 as the Internal Revenue Code of 1986.

HISTORY OF TOP INDIVIDUAL TAX RATES
[Selected Years]

YEAR	TOP RATE	YEAR	TOP RATE
1913	7%	1936	79%
1916	15%	1944	94%
1917	67%	1950	91%
1918	77%	1965	70%
1922	56%	1969	77%
1924	46%	1982	50%
1925	25%	New Law	28%
1932	63%		

Fairness—A Guiding Force Behind Tax Reform

Perhaps the overriding philosophical goal of the tax reform effort was to make the tax system "fairer." It was an effort to redesign the system so that people of similar incomes would pay a similar amount of taxes. No longer would your neighbor with a shrewd tax adviser or a profitable corporation with a team of tax experts be able to escape paying a "fair" share of taxes. In large measure, the tax overhaul was driven by the precept that providing special exemptions for certain classes of taxpayers only increases the tax burden on all others.

"We succeeded only because we never forgot that the ultimate measure of tax policy—on Capitol Hill and along Main Street—is fairness," said Representative Dan Rostenkowski, the Chicago Democrat who is chairman of the House Ways and Means Committee. "It is the single promise that generated what tentative public support the president was able to generate. It wasn't low tax rates or larger paychecks that brought working men and women behind tax reform. It was fairness—knowing they weren't subsidizing a loophole for the guy down the street, or the corporation across town."

"Without fairness and the perception of fairness, our system of voluntary compliance falls apart," said Senate Majority Leader Bob Dole of Kansas. Added Senator Bob Packwood, the Oregon Republican who was chairman of the Senate Finance Committee, moments before the final vote on the tax reform bill: "Taxes are about more than money; they are about more than economics. They are about fairness—and this bill is fair."

Fairness was as much an issue in the redesign of the corporate tax system as it was in the restructuring of the individual income tax. Congress sought to level the playing field for business, ending many of the special tax preferences that favored one industry over another.

Other objectives of the tax reform effort, such as making the system simpler, often took a backseat in the interest of fairness. For example, many provisions contain complicated phase-outs and exceptions because Congress wanted to give people some time to adjust to the tax changes, such as was the case with the consumer-interest deduction. Rather than repealing the deduction overnight, it is phased out over a four-year period.

Certainly, the new tax law fell far short of being perfectly fair. Many members of Congress complained that some of the provisions unfairly changed the rules in the middle of the game. For example, some considered it unfair that previously made student loans were not exempted from the repeal of the consumer-interest deduction. Others thought it unfair that homeowners were given a way to circumvent the new restrictions on interest deductions while renters were not.

Some industries that had strong supporters among tax writers, such as oil and gas, got to retain most of their special tax breaks, while other industries were forced to give theirs up.

To be sure, fairness is a subjective term. What one person regards as a loophole is another's cherished tax benefit. But if the definition of fairness is to make for a more level playing field, the new system goes far toward achieving that goal. As evidence, one merely has to observe how far rates were lowered to see how far Congress went to eliminate the special exceptions that had long been a part of the tax code.

How Tax Reform May Simplify Your Life

One of the chief objectives of the tax reform effort was to make the tax system simpler. After glancing at the sweeping changes embodied in the new law, however, most people might well conclude that tax reform will do nothing but further complicate their lives and make filing their tax returns an even more agonizing annual ritual.

Was the original goal of simplifying the tax system abandoned in the heap of backroom political compromises? Did Congress's effort to appease many interests and go only halfway in curtailing certain tax deductions create a system that is even more confusing and more complex?

The answer is that while Congress could have gone much further to simplify the system, the seeming patchwork actually makes great inroads in removing some of the layers of complexity that have so frustrated taxpayers on April 15 and encouraged many to spend countless hours the rest of the year in search of ways to save on taxes.

To be sure, Congress lacked the political appetite for a wholesale cleanup of tax benefits needed to make the system as simple as you probably expected. But for the vast majority of American households the system will be somewhat simpler.

Even for those taxpayers who might find filling out their tax return a more perplexing and time-consuming affair, the new system will diminish the role that taxes play in their lives the rest of the year. With dozens of tax benefits curtailed or eliminated outright, and the value of most others sharply reduced by the lower tax rates, the importance of taxes in investment decisions will be reduced. So will the incentive to look for ways to beat the system and shelter income from the tax collector.

"The major simplification has nothing to do with the return itself," says Henry Aaron, a leading authority on taxes and a senior fellow at the Brookings Institution, a Washington think tank. "If one wants to look where the tax code complicates people's lives, it's more on the effect of transactions that people engage in three hundred sixty-five days a year, rather than the one day a year they spend filling out a tax return. By treating capital gains as ordinary income and simply getting rid of a lot of itemized deductions and credits, somewhat fewer calculations need to be made when people decide to go out the front door to work, to put up a building, or to buy a capital asset."

Tax return forms are not likely to be much shorter. But more taxpayers are likely to join the ranks of those who are already able to take advantage of the short and simple 1040A and 1040EZ tax return forms.

By sharply increasing the standard deduction and curtailing a number of popular itemized deductions, the non-itemizer population is expected to swell to as high as 70 percent or 75 percent of American households, up from about 62 percent under the old law.

LESS RECORD KEEPING, FEWER CALCULATIONS, FEWER IRS DISPUTES

For taxpayers who will still be itemizing their deductions, the repeal of the state and local sales tax deduction will eliminate the need to save sales receipts. It will also end the need to engage in the year-end tactic of trying to accelerate major purchases in order to generate a larger sales tax deduction. Since miscellaneous itemized deductions and most employee business expenses will be deductible only to the extent that they exceed 2 percent of adjusted gross income, people who never incur enough of these types of expenses simply will no longer care about the deduction and stop keeping records.

Some complex computations will also be eliminated. For instance, the repeal of income averaging as a method for figuring tax liability will eliminate an extra calculation that many individuals were advised to make each year. The repeal of the two-earner marriage deduction and the partial exclusion for unemployment compensation will rid the code of two more calculations.

In addition, some of the deductions that have been a source of constant litigious debate between the Internal Revenue Service and taxpayers—such as the educational travel deduction for teachers, capital-gains and tax-shelter deductions—will be eliminated.

Condensing the fourteen-to-fifteen bracket system to two rates (three if you count a 33-percent rate that upper-income taxpayers will face on part of their income) will make it easier for you to know what tax bracket you are in when considering the tax consequences of investments, such as the after-tax cost of buying a home. Under the old law, few people knew what their tax bracket really was.

THE REMAINING LOOPHOLES ARE NOT AS FRUITFUL

Certainly, not every loophole was closed by the new tax law. There will still be some strategies around for those intent on finding ways to save on taxes. But these efforts will not be as effective or as widely applicable as those that are curtailed by the new law. This will go far toward simplifying the system for a great many taxpayers. Under the old law, many people felt they needed to be tax lawyers, or at least needed to hire one, in order to make sure they were not missing out on any of the multitude of tax benefits. They also felt compelled to plan all their financial affairs based on the latest tax-saving strategies. With many tax benefits curtailed and so many tax-saving schemes rendered extinct or much less valuable, most people will no longer feel like they are missing out on as much if they aren't tax lawyers. People who simply want to work at their jobs and don't want to invest in tax shelters or play other tax games won't be losing as much under the new law. "There's a tremendous lowering of the penalty for not having a taste for tax planning," said Michael J. Graetz, a professor at the Yale Law School and a former Treasury attorney.

MORE COMPLEX FOR SOME—PARTICULARLY AT THE BEGINNING

Admittedly, not everyone will find the system simpler, either in filling out their tax return forms or in their daily lives. For example, the new restrictions on consumer-interest deductions may cause new headaches and some rejuggling of finances by people with large amounts of outstanding debt. Similarly, many middle-income taxpayers will not know until year end how much of a tax deduction they will receive from Individual Retirement Account contributions because of the new income guidelines.

Initially, most taxpayers are bound to find the new system more complicated and confusing as they try to absorb the new rules and adjust their financial affairs. Part of the complexity will result from the phase-in of a number of provisions. For instance, the repeal of the deduction for consumer interest will be gradually phased in over a period of years, requiring different calculations each year.

Early on, accountants and lawyers are likely to be swamped with clients who are confused by the new rules and need help adjusting their financial affairs. After a time, however, many people might feel less need for professional help, since tax-planning efforts would no longer be as fruitful with the top rate lowered to 28-percent and many effective tax-saving strategies gone.

Undoubtedly, there will be people who will still cling to their advisers because their financial affairs are so wide-ranging or because they think that paying taxes at a 28-percent rate is still a significant sum and only slightly less abhorrent than paying taxes at a 50-percent rate.

"The trouble is that tax planning for many high-income individuals has been as much a part of their life as having a drink or going to the movies," said Mr. Graetz. "Once you've been addicted, it's a monkey on your back that's going to be hard to shed."

How Tax Reform Will Affect the Economy

Over the long term, many economists believe that the new tax law will lead to a healthier economy. Few expect any economic miracles. And all emphasize the difficulty of predicting the impact of legislation that is so sweeping in scope.

But many economists see the new law fostering more productive investment, thereby enhancing the prospects for economic growth.

The theory is that free-market forces—rather than government-chosen tax incentives—can best guide where the nation's scarce economic resources should be invested. The patchwork of tax incentives of the old law, many economists contend, led to billions of dollars of misallocated resources. The tax system nourished tax shelters and other wasteful investments at the expense of ventures that offer greater prospects for growth. Economists often cite the glut of Houston office buildings as evidence that the old tax system encouraged resources to flow into activities that would otherwise be unprofitable except for the tax benefits. While these buildings may have provided the economy with extra jobs during construction, they offer no long-term job opportunities if they sit vacant or half empty. The new law, by removing the tax incentives that favored one activity over another, is designed to allow free-market forces to steer money, labor, and materials to their most productive uses.

Many economists believe the new law will also bring about lower interest rates because of the tight restrictions placed on deductions for consumer borrowing.

But not all economists see a brighter future under the new law. By scaling back investment incentives and increasing the tax burden on business, some economists fear business investment will decline, thereby reducing long-term economic growth. They say the new law will hit hardest the backbone of American industry, heavy manufacturing, and erode America's competitive position in the world marketplace.

But many tax economists are skeptical that investment tax incentives have significantly helped achieve a higher level of investment in this country. They contend that most business investment decisions aren't made on the basis of tax benefits, but rather because demand for their product requires expanding their facilities or because buying new equipment will enhance productivity.

Although business will have a heavier tax burden to bear, consumers will have more money in their pockets to spend and invest, which in turn could help stimulate business. General Motors, for one, thought the individual tax cuts would help increase their car sales, and more than offset any business tax breaks they would lose.

CONCERN IN THE SHORT TERM

Even economists who see long-term benefits from the new tax law are concerned about the short-term impact of the tax changes as the economy makes the transition. Companies that will be hurt by the tax bill are likely to react first, cutting back on investment, while companies that will benefit from the new law are likely to take longer to step up their investments. Canceling plans for an investment can be done instantly, while planning new investments can take months or years. The Reagan administration contends any short-run negative effects will be small and can be absorbed by the economy without serious risk.

"Supply-Side" Economics—A Driving Force

Certainly a driving force behind President Reagan's push for tax reform is his belief in "supply-side" economics. According to this school of economic philosophy, lowering tax rates will lead Americans to work harder, save more, and invest more, and thereby launch the economy on a course of long-term, noninflationary growth.

Indeed, Mr. Reagan has ascribed the economic expansion after the 1981–82 recession in large part to his 1981 tax-cut program, which lowered tax rates across the board and brought the top rate down from 70 percent to 50 percent.

Supply-side theory holds that the lower the "marginal" tax rate—the top rate at which your income is taxed; that is, the rate on an extra dollar of income earned—the bigger your after-tax, or take-home, dollar, and the more incentive you have to work and save more. The supply-side impact of tax-rate reductions is greatest for those in the highest income brackets. The incentive effects diminish as you move into the lower income brackets.

What this means is that if you are facing a 50-percent marginal rate, for example, you might not be too motivated to work overtime or take on a second job, since the federal government would be taking half of whatever extra you earn. If you get to keep only half the fruits of your labors, you might decide that working overtime is not worth the effort. Similarly, you might be discouraged from saving or investing a lot of money because half the earnings would be taxed away. Instead you might be encouraged to just spend it or invest it in a tax shelter or some other place where the income could be shielded from the tax collector.

But if the top rate was lowered to 28 percent, according to the theory, you might well be encouraged to take on extra work because you would get to keep 72 cents of every extra dollar you earn, instead of 50 cents. A non-working spouse might also be encouraged to take on a job, since more money would be brought home. In addition, you would have greater incentive to save more and have less incentive to try to find ways to shelter income from taxes.

Will these lower rates, then, unleash a fury of economic growth and create a nation of people who work much harder and save much more? Most economists do not share the optimism of supply-side disciples, such as California economist Arthur Laffer, whose theories helped pave the way for the 1981 tax cuts. Rather, the mainstream view holds that lowering marginal rates will have only a small incentive effect on work and saving.

Will Higher Corporate Taxes Affect Individuals?

No doubt many Americans are very happy about the prospect that corporations will be shouldering a bigger share of the income tax burden under the new law, giving individuals some welcome relief. But some economists and corporate lobbyists are of the view that individuals will end up paying the corporate tab one way or another. Their refrain: Corporations do not bear the burden of higher taxes, only people do.

What they mean is that corporations simply will pass the extra tax on to consumers in the form of higher retail prices. Or the extra tax will force corporations to tighten their belts and either lay off employees or pay them less. Or shareholders will suffer because profits will be reduced. Exactly where the burden falls, and in what form or combination of forms, is a much-debated issue among tax scholars.

A corporation facing an increase in corporate taxes under the new law might well try to pass the extra cost on to consumers. But not all companies will be able to do so. Companies facing stiff foreign competition, for example, will have great difficulty raising their prices. The same would be true for companies selling products whose demand is sensitive to price changes. If they raise prices, they will lose some customers. Or customers will not buy as much of that product. In these cases, the tax increase would likely result in smaller profit margins for the company, which will either hurt stockholders or force the company to cut back on its expenses.

But keep in mind that not every corporation will see its tax bill increase under the new law. Many, such as retailers and food processors, will face significant tax reductions. As a result, their profit margins will initially rise, providing greater rewards for stockholders and perhaps employees. With increased profit margins, new competition will be attracted to these businesses, which would benefit consumers.

The New Tax Law and Your Savings

The new law scales back many of the special tax breaks that were intended to encourage Americans to save. The tax deduction for Individual Retirement Accounts, for instance, will pass into extinction for millions of middle- and upper-income taxpayers who are covered by some sort of retirement plan at work. The new law also limits the amount of money people can contribute to 401(k)s and other employer-sponsored retirement plans to defer taxes. And parents will find that the savings accounts of their younger children are subject to harsher tax rules.

To be sure, some economists and politicians questioned the wisdom of cutting back all these special tax incentives, particularly when the nation's savings rate was already so low. But many economists believe that the lower individual tax rates will help encourage savings and offset the loss of the special tax incentives. You will have less of your interest and dividends taxed away each year. And the reduced rate applies to all of your money, not just the limited amounts that were eligible for the special tax breaks. So while you might lose the old deduction for the $2,000 or so you stashed away in an Individual Retirement Account each year, the rest of your savings will be taxed at much lower rates than before.

In addition, not all the special tax breaks are gone. Even people who lose the IRA deduction will still be able to put money into an IRA, where it can grow and compound tax-free until withdrawn. And while contribution limits to employer-sponsored savings plans were reduced, only a small percentage of people ever contributed more than the new limits allow.

All is not lost for children's savings accounts either. The first $1,000 a year of investment income earned by young children will still be taxed at the child's rates rather than the parents' rates. And children fourteen or older will continue to have all of their income taxed at their own low rate.

3

INDIVIDUAL TAX CUTS

The Size of Your Tax Cut

A majority of taxpayers will see their federal income tax bills go down by a few hundred dollars or even a few thousand dollars under the new law. When the new tax system is fully in place in 1988, tax bills will be reduced by an average 6.1 percent. Every income group will get a tax cut. But the size of the reduction will vary sharply according to income class and from individual to individual, depending on their financial circumstances. About one in six taxpayers will see their taxes go up.

The Congressional Joint Committee on Taxation estimates that about 58 percent of taxpayers will get a tax cut, 15.5 percent will see their taxes increase, and 26.5 percent will see no change.

Likely to get hit with a tax increase are those who invested in tax shelters or had substantial amounts of capital-gains income, which will be taxed more harshly under the new law. Also hit will be people who took significant advantage of the many deductions that will be curtailed under the new law.

People who don't itemize their deductions or who made relatively little use of the tax benefits now to be curtailed will generally see their taxes reduced.

UPPER-INCOME TAXPAYERS

In percentage terms, upper-income taxpayers earning more than $50,000 a year will receive the smallest tax cut, ranging from 1.2 percent to 2.4 percent. But in dollar terms they will receive the biggest tax cut, ranging from more than $1,000 for taxpayers earning between $50,000 and $75,000 to more than a $50,000 tax cut for people earning over $200,000.

TAX CUTS AND INCREASES IN 1988

INCOME CLASS	PERCENTAGE OF TAXPAYERS WITH TAX INCREASE*	AVERAGE INCREASE	PERCENTAGE OF TAXPAYERS WITH TAX DECREASE*	AVERAGE DECREASE
$0–$10,000	4%	$ 214	28%	$ 170
$10,001–$20,000	14%	$ 235	75%	$ 310
$20,001–$30,000	21%	$ 346	75%	$ 390
$30,001–$40,000	25%	$ 554	74%	$ 554
$40,001–$50,000	20%	$ 926	80%	$ 841
$50,001–$75,000	37%	$ 1,378	62%	$ 1,066
$75,001–$100,000	37%	$ 3,120	61%	$ 2,187
$100,001–$200,000	37%	$ 8,312	63%	$ 5,803
Over $200,000	44%	$55,700	56%	$50,122

* Represents percentage of total taxpayers in the respective income category. Total taxpayers includes both filers and non-filers and includes returns with no change in liability.
SOURCE: Data from estimates by Joint Committee on Taxation

Some liberal Democrats were critical of this fact, arguing that wealthy people should not receive another windfall after the big tax cut they got from the 1981 Tax Act, which lowered the top rate from 70 percent to 50 percent. But in designing a system that sharply lowered rates there was no way to avoid some of these large windfalls among the wealthy. Most of the wealthy who will receive the huge tax cuts are those who have not been heavily sheltering their income and thus have generally been paying a relatively substantial amount of taxes. Furthermore, about half the people in the over-$200,000 income class will see their taxes increase sharply, by an average of $55,700.

Of those earning between $50,000 and $200,000, more than one in three taxpayers will see their taxes increase, a much larger proportion than in the lower- and middle-income classes.

MIDDLE-INCOME TAXPAYERS

Congressional tax writers wanted to make sure that the lion's share of the more than $120 billion in individual tax cuts went to lower- and middle-income taxpayers. And most of the money was earmarked for those income groups.

People earning between $20,000 and $30,000 will receive a tax cut averaging 9.8 percent; those earning between $30,000 and $40,000, 7.7 percent; and between $40,000 and $50,000, 9.1 percent. In dollar terms, the average annual tax cuts range from $390 to $841.

Winners among the middle class will far exceed the number of losers. Between 75 percent and 80 percent of middle-income taxpayers will see their taxes reduced.

LOW-INCOME INDIVIDUALS

In percentage terms, the lowest income groups will receive the largest tax cuts, with about 6 million families living at or below the poverty line being completely removed from the income tax rolls. A family of four would be able to earn more than $15,000 in 1988 before it owed a cent in federal income taxes, compared to less than $10,000 under the old law. A single person would not be subject to federal income tax until his earnings exceeded $4,950.

People earning under $10,000 a year will see their taxes drop by 65.1 percent, while those earning between $10,000 and $20,000 will see their tax bill decline by 22.3 percent. The average income tax cut will range from $170 to $310. According to an analysis by the Center on Budget and Policy Priorities, a Washington, D.C.-based research organization, the new tax law will reduce the combined federal income and payroll tax burden on a family of four earning poverty-level wages by more than $1,000.

Tax relief will not be as substantial for single taxpayers, though most of them will pay less than they did under the old law. However, some single individuals below the poverty line will not be removed from the tax rolls. While Congress expressed concern about this, tax writers noted that low-income single individuals tend to be young and often either live with their parents or receive significant financial help from their families.

MORE TAXPAYERS FACE TAX INCREASES IN 1987

Some taxpayers who will get a tax cut when the new system is fully in place may be in for an unpleasant surprise when they fill out their 1987 tax returns in early 1988—a tax increase.

The reason is that while most tax benefits are curtailed beginning in 1987, tax rates are not fully lowered until 1988. As a result, people who are in the top brackets will lose the benefit of their deductions in 1987 while gaining only part of the benefit of lower rates.

Upper-income taxpayers will be affected most. On average, people earning above $75,000 will see their tax bills increase by more than 4 percent in 1987. People earning over $200,000 will see their tax bills go up almost 10 percent.

People earning between $50,000 and $75,000 will get a tax cut of about 1 percent. But most people earning below $50,000 will receive substantial tax cuts beginning on their 1987 returns, which are due April 15, 1988. Others will have to wait until they fill out their 1988 returns in early 1989.

HOW THE TAX CUTS MEASURE UP
BY INCOME GROUP

INCOME CLASS*	PERCENTAGE CHANGE IN TAX LIABILITY	
	1987	*1988*
Less than $10,000	− 57.2%	− 65.1%
$10,001–$20,000	− 16.7%	− 22.3%
$20,001–$30,000	− 10.8%	− 9.8%
$30,001–$40,000	− 9.4%	− 7.7%
$40,001–$50,000	− 9.8%	− 9.1%
$50,001–$75,000	− 1.0%	− 1.8%
$75,001–$100,000	+ 4.3%	− 1.2%
$100,001–$200,000	+ 4.6%	− 2.2%
$200,001 and above	+ 9.8%	− 2.4%
TOTAL	− 2.2%	− 6.1%

* 1986 dollars
SOURCE: Joint Committee on Taxation

4

TAX-SAVING STRATEGIES

Long-Term Strategies

With the rules of the game so dramatically changed, the new tax law will require new strategies and a new way of thinking when it comes to financial and investment decisions. Following are some suggestions.

• Keep in mind the dramatically reduced benefit that tax benefits will now provide. Many of them have been eliminated outright or sharply curtailed. But even where a tax deduction is preserved intact, its value is sharply diminished by the lower tax rates. This may take some getting used to because deductions haven't been worth less in more than fifty years. That's how long it has been since tax rates were so low. What this means is that such expenditures as employee business expenses, consumer loan interest, and real estate investments will no longer be as heavily subsidized by the government. More of these expenses will have to come out of your own pocket. The same is true when it comes to the government helping subsidize your losses whether they be casualty and theft losses or business losses. The tax system can no longer be counted on to help cushion the losses as much as in the past.

• Don't be afraid of earning more money. Under the old law, some people hesitated when it came to working overtime, taking on an extra job, or getting into an investment that generated a lot of income. They complained that the extra money would simply push them into a higher tax bracket and the federal government would end up taking away up to half of it. But under the new law, the balance has shifted. With tax rates so sharply reduced, you get to keep most of what you make. The fruits of your successes will be largely yours to keep and do with as you wish.

• Reassess the merits of each investment in light of the tax changes. Their

24

relative appeal is marginally changed in some cases and dramatically changed in others. Investments that used to carry enticing tax advantages may no longer be enticing at all.

• Focus on the economic soundness of the investment rather than tax benefits. Under the old law, tax benefits could sometimes make an otherwise unprofitable venture profitable. But under the new law, tax write-offs will no longer be enough to bail out a marginal deal. If an office building sits half empty, investors are going to lose money. Tax savings will no longer make up for the operating losses.

• You will hear many brokers and salesmen touting investments whose tax advantages were preserved. For example, municipal bonds are being promoted as one of the few tax shelters left. But their tax advantages, while important, are not as valuable as they used to be because of the lower tax rates. They may still be attractive, particularly if municipal bond yields adjust to compensate for the impact of the tax changes. But you're going to have to make some calculations. In comparing investments, always compare the returns after taxes.

• Keep in mind that consumer purchases—be it a car or a refrigerator—get more expensive under the new law. State and local sales taxes will no longer be deductible. And if you finance the purchase by credit card or through consumer loans, the deduction for interest is phased out. Thus, you will no longer have the federal government helping finance your spending.

• Try to reduce your outstanding credit card balances and other consumer debt. With the interest deduction phased out, your outstanding balances become more expensive to maintain. If you need to borrow money, consider the types of loans where the interest deductions are still available, such as home loans.

• Reassess your savings for retirement under the new law. If you are no longer eligible to claim a deduction for Individual Retirement Accounts, explore your options. If you have a 401(k) employee retirement plan at work, the plan will provide you with the same tax advantages as the IRA used to. If you don't find a suitable option, you will have to make do with what's available, such as the nondeductible IRA, or investing outside a special retirement program. But don't reduce the amount you are putting away for retirement just because a particular tax-saving program has been eliminated or reduced. When you retire, you may end up blaming Congress for your lack of retirement savings, but you will be the one who suffers.

Tax-Saving Steps to Take Before the New Law Becomes Fully Effective

Before the provisions of the new law become fully effective, some last-chance opportunities exist to take advantage of tax benefits before they vanish or become diminished in value under the new law. At the same time, there are strategies that will allow you to take maximum advantage of the new lower rates that will be in effect under the new law.

CHARITABLE CONTRIBUTIONS: Be extra generous in the remaining days of 1986, rather than wait to make your charitable donation in 1987 or later. The charity will certainly appreciate having the gift early, and you will receive the benefit of a bigger deduction. Nonitemizers won't be able to claim a charitable deduction after 1986. And the itemized deduction will be worth less in 1987 because of the lower tax rates, and even less in 1988 when tax rates are fully lowered. Upper-income taxpayers who donate stock, real estate, artwork, and other appreciated property have another reason for giving in 1986: Part of the charitable deduction for gifts of appreciated property becomes subject to the alternative minimum tax beginning in 1987.

BIG-TICKET PURCHASES: If you are planning to purchase a car, boat, plane, motorcycle, truck or motor home, consider buying it before the end of 1986. By so doing, you could take advantage of the itemized sales tax deduction, which will be gone in 1987.

EMPLOYEE BUSINESS EXPENSES AND MISCELLANEOUS ITEMIZED DEDUCTIONS: Beginning in 1987, these expenses will be deductible only to the extent they exceed 2 percent of adjusted gross income. As a result, consider paying for as many of these expenses as possible in 1986, including professional association dues and subscriptions to professional and investment publications. But be aware that if you prepay expenses too far in advance, such as trying to take out a ten-year subscription, the IRS may try to challenge the write-off. "You're going to push the IRS to the point of questioning reasonableness," said Jeff J. Saccacio, national director of personal financial planning at the accounting firm of KMG Main Hurdman. "It's the old syndrome: If you're a pig you're going to get caught."

SETTLE TAX DISPUTES: Pay off any interest charges owed the IRS before the end of 1986, when the interest will still be fully deductible. "You ought to settle contests with the IRS if you can settle sensibly," said Albert Ellentuck, national tax partner at the accounting firm of Laventhol & Horwath.

ESTIMATED STATE TAX PAYMENTS: Prepay before the end of the year any 1986 estimated state and local taxes that may not be due until early 1987. By paying before the end of 1986 you will be able to claim the state and local tax deduction in 1986 when the deduction is worth more because of the higher tax rates. "The only caveat is that you can't make a wildly out-of-line estimate," said Mr. Saccacio of Main Hurdman. "It has to be reasonable." In other words, the IRS does not look kindly on people who try to greatly inflate their estimated tax payments in order to inflate the deduction.

MEDICAL EXPENSES: Get your regular medical and dental checkups before the end of 1986. If you're planning on having elective surgery performed, consider scheduling and paying for it before the end of 1986. In 1987 the itemized deduction for medical expenses will be harder to obtain and less rewarding for those who do qualify.

CONTRIBUTING TO RETIREMENT ACCOUNTS: All workers will still be allowed to claim a deduction on their 1986 tax returns for contributions made to Individual Retirement Accounts. The deduction doesn't get restricted until the 1987 tax year. You have until April 15, 1987, to make the contribution and claim the deduction.

BUYING BUSINESS EQUIPMENT: If you own your own business, consider buying business equipment before the end of 1986—be it a computer, a car, a copy machine, etc. You won't be able to claim an investment tax credit, since it was retroactively abolished to the beginning of 1986. But the value of the first-year depreciation write-offs will be more valuable in 1986, since rates are higher. In addition, some of the depreciation schedules of the old law provide a much bigger benefit than the new law. That is the case with business automobiles. In any event, you generally have the option of using either the old or new depreciation schedules for property placed in service between August 1, 1986, and the end of 1986.

POLITICAL CONTRIBUTIONS: If you intend to contribute to a political campaign, consider doing it in 1986 because the political contributions tax credit will be gone in 1987.

DEFER INCOME: Where possible, try to defer income to a future year when rates are lower. Employees could try to arrange with their bosses to have their year-end bonuses paid in January instead of December. If you own your own business, you might consider delaying sending out year-end bills until the first of the year.

Investors can move money out of bank accounts or money market funds, where interest accrues daily, and invest it in Treasury bills or certificates of deposit that mature after December 31, 1986. By so doing, interest income will not be recognized for tax purposes until 1987 when rates are lower. These same strategies can be used again at the end of 1987 so that the income will be taxed at the lower 1988 rates.

STRATEGIES FOR UPPER-INCOME TAXPAYERS SUBJECT TO THE MINIMUM TAX

Not everyone will be better off accelerating deductions and deferring income. Upper-income taxpayers who fall prey to the alternative minimum tax would generally be better off realizing income in 1986, when it would be taxed at the 20 percent minimum tax rate. Similarly, they may be better off not trying to accelerate deductions into 1986, because most deductions are disallowed under the minimum tax computation and those that are allowed would be worth no more than 20 percent.

SELLING APPRECIATED ASSETS

If you have stocks or other assets that have appreciated in value and that you are thinking of unloading, consider selling them before the end of 1986 while the top rate on long-term capital gains is still 20 percent. Long-term capital gains get taxed at rates of up to 28 percent in 1987 and up to 33 percent thereafter.

But don't dump an asset just because of the tax. If you think an asset still has room to appreciate, the future gain may more than offset the extra tax you may have to pay if you sell later. Plus you'll be able to delay having to pay the tax.

If you have a big gain in a stock and you still like its prospects, you can sell the shares and turn right around and reinvest in the same stock. By so doing, you can lock in your gain and pay tax on it at the lower 1986 capital-gains rate. The cost: brokerage commissions. In addition, the tax will be due by April 15, 1987. If you don't have the money to pay the tax, you can use some of the proceeds from the sale of the stock and simply buy fewer shares back. Before executing the sale, make sure your tax savings will more than offset the brokerage commissions. Keep in mind that favorable long-term capital-gains treatment applies only to stock and other assets held longer than six months.

If you purchased stock since July 1, 1986, you will pay less tax by waiting until 1987 to sell. If you sold the shares in 1986, they would be short-term gains and subject to tax at regular rates of up to 50 percent. If you sell in 1987, they will be taxed at lower rates.

If you're selling investment real estate to take last-minute advantage of the lower capital-gains rate, be aware that you may be selling into a declining market. Investment real-estate prices have declined in many parts of the country in the rush to sell before capital-gains treatment comes to an end. You'll have to judge whether it might pay to hold off until the selling pressure eases. If you wait, you might be able to get a better price that will more than offset any extra tax you would have to pay by waiting. But you'll have to make the assessment to see if its worth sacrificing this last-chance opportunity to take advantage of the lower capital-gains rate.

Also keep in mind that if you used accelerated depreciation to write off your real-estate property, part of your gain may be subject to regular tax rates, rather than capital-gains rates. If the portion subject to regular rates is a large chunk of your total gain, you might be better off waiting to sell until regular tax rates are lowered in 1987, says Byrle M. Abbin, managing director of the office of federal tax services at the accounting firm Arthur Andersen & Company. But you'll have to make the calculation to determine the timing that gives you the most tax saving.

If you plan to buy a rental property, you might try to do so before the end of 1986 in order to qualify for a more generous depreciation write-off schedule. Residential rental properties placed in service by December 31, 1986, can be written off over 19 years, compared to 27.5 years under the new law. People who are looking for investment real estate may find some attractive bargains because of the rush by owners to unload investment properties. "Whenever someone has a problem, there's an opportunity for someone else," said Herbert Paul, a New York tax attorney.

5

THE NEW TAX SYSTEM

The New Tax Rate System: An Overview

The focal point of the new tax law is the vastly streamlined system of tax rates. The old system of fourteen or fifteen rate brackets ranging from 11 percent to 50 percent is replaced by two rate brackets, 15 percent and 28 percent. Effectively, there is also a higher "hidden" rate of 33 percent that upper-income taxpayers will pay on part of their income. More on that later.

Over 80 percent of taxpayers will fall into the 15-percent rate bracket. A family of four claiming just the standard deduction and personal exemptions could earn as much as $42,550 in 1988 and still be in the 15-percent bracket. If the family claimed other deductions, they could earn even more before being pushed into the 28-percent bracket. An unmarried head of household with two children could have gross income up to $34,150 without claiming any special deductions and still be in the 15-percent bracket. A single taxpayer could earn up to $22,800 before reaching the 28-percent bracket.

The 28-percent tax bracket does not kick in until taxable income (your income figure after adjustments, deductions, and personal exemptions) reaches $29,750 on joint returns, $23,900 for heads of household, $17,850 for single individuals, and $14,875 for married persons filing separate returns.

Do not be too alarmed if your income slips past the threshold and you are pushed into the 28-percent bracket. All your income will not suddenly be taxed at 28-percent. Only the amount that exceeds the income threshold for the 28-percent bracket will be taxed at 28 percent. The rest will be taxed at the 15-percent rate. For example, consider a married couple with taxable income of $30,000. On a joint return, the threshold for the 28-percent bracket is $29,750. So the first $29,750 of the couple's income would be taxed at 15 percent, and only the remaining $250 would be taxed at 28 percent.

The old tax system operated in similar fashion. Millionaires had the first dollars of their income taxed at the same low rates as poor people.

Upper-Income Taxpayers and the Hidden 33-Percent Rate

What makes the new system different is that some upper-income taxpayers will not have the benefit of having their first dollars of income taxed at 15 percent. The benefit of the 15-percent tax bracket is phased out for income above certain levels. Why? Congress wanted to lower tax rates as far as possible, but they needed to find some way to prevent upper-income taxpayers from reaping a huge windfall from the sharp cut in the top tax rate to 28 percent. The benefit of the 15-percent tax bracket starts to phase out when taxable income exceeds $71,900 on a joint return, $61,650 on a head-of-household return, $43,150 on single returns, and $35,950 for a married person filing separately.

The phase-out is gradual. A surcharge of 5 percent is added to income above the threshold income levels. As a result of this surcharge, income above the threshold is effectively taxed at a marginal rate of 33 percent (28 percent plus the 5 percent surcharge), rather than 28 percent. This is the hidden 33-percent rate mentioned earlier. The phase-out of the 15-percent bracket benefit is completed when taxable income reaches $149,250 on a joint return, $123,790 for head of household, $89,560 on a single return, and $113,300 for a married person filing separately.

Thus, if your income was exactly $149,250 on a joint return, you would effectively have all of it taxed at a flat 28-percent rate, since the benefit of the 15-percent bracket would be completely eliminated. If your income was somewhere in between $71,900 and $149,250, it would be taxed at an overall rate of something less than 28 percent, since the surcharge would not have yet canceled out all the benefit of the 15-percent bracket.

PHASE-OUT OF PERSONAL EXEMPTIONS KEEPS TOP RATE AT 33 PERCENT

After the 15-percent bracket is phased out, the wealthiest taxpayers have one more surcharge to contend with. This time, the 5-percent surcharge is intended to phase out the benefit of the personal exemptions. The new surcharge begins where the other left off—i.e., at $149,250 on a joint return, $123,790 for head of household, $89,560 on a single return, and $113,300 for a married person filing separately.

This surcharge works the same way as the one that applied to the phase-out of the 15-percent tax bracket. The 5-percent surcharge is applied to income above the thresholds (e.g., $149,250 on a joint return). The phase-out continues until the value of all your personal exemptions is wiped out. At what income level the phase-out is completed will vary according to the number of exemptions you have. For a family of four, the phase-out of their four personal exemptions would be completed when taxable income reaches $192,930 on a joint return in 1988. For a family of five, the phase-out would not be completed until income reached $203,850. (Each exemption takes $10,920 of taxable income to phase out in 1988 when personal exemptions are $1,950; in 1989, when personal exemptions are $2,000, each exemption is phased out over an $11,200 income range.) For single taxpayers, the phase-out of their one personal exemption would be completed when income reached $100,480 in 1988, and $100,760 in 1989. (Do not worry about the mathematics of all this. The IRS is likely to incorporate the surcharges in tables beginning with 1988 tax returns, when the phase-outs first apply.)

Once the phase-outs are completed, no further surcharges apply. Therefore, the marginal tax rate on additional taxable income (e.g., beyond $192,930 for a family of four) would drop back to 28 percent.

To summarize, this family of four would find the first $29,750 of their taxable income taxed at a marginal rate of 15 percent, and between $29,750 and $71,900 at a 28-percent rate. Between $71,900 and $192,930, income will be taxed at a marginal rate of 33 percent. Income in excess of $192,930 would be taxed at a marginal rate of 28 percent.

The bottom-line effect of all this is to make the highest-income people pay tax on their total taxable income at a rate slightly in excess of 28 percent. While the phase-out of the 15-percent bracket makes for a flat 28-percent rate, the phase-out of the personal exemptions pushes the effective rate over the 28-percent line. For a family of four with $192,930 in income, the effective rate would be about 29.1 percent. For a millionaire, the effective rate would be just over 28 percent, since most of his income would be taxed at 28 percent and only a relatively small amount would be taxed at 33 percent.

Tax Rates for the 1987 Transition Year

The new two-bracket tax system (with the hidden third bracket of 33 percent) does not go into full effect until 1988. Because of revenue considerations, Congress decided to make 1987 a transition year, blending the old tax rates and the new tax rates into a five-bracket system for the one year only. The rates are 11 percent, 15 percent, 28 percent, 35 percent, and 38.5 percent.

For 1987 there are no surcharges in effect for upper-income taxpayers. So they get to keep the benefit of all of their personal exemptions, as well as the benefit of the lower rate brackets.

If you look at the 1987 tax tables, you will see that the top bracket of 38.5 percent kicks in for taxable income in excess of $90,000 on a joint return, $80,000 for heads of household, $54,000 for single returns, and $45,000 for married persons filing separately. By comparison, people with income in excess of these thresholds would have been in at least the 42-percent tax bracket (45-percent bracket for heads of household) on their 1986 tax returns.

TAX RATES FOR INDIVIDUALS
FILING SINGLE RETURNS

1986

TAXABLE INCOME	MARGINAL RATE	TAXABLE INCOME	MARGINAL RATE
0–$2,480	0%	$16,190–$19,640	23%
$2,480–$3,670	11%	$19,640–$25,360	26%
$3,670–$4,750	12%	$25,360–$31,080	30%
$4,750–$7,010	14%	$31,080–$36,800	34%
$7,010–$9,170	15%	$36,800–$44,780	38%
$9,170–$11,650	16%	$44,780–$59,670	42%
$11,650–$13,920	18%	$59,670–$88,270	48%
$13,920–$16,190	20%	Over $88,270	50%

NOTE: 1986 tax-rate tables set by old law

TAX RATES FOR INDIVIDUALS
FILING SINGLE RETURNS

	1987*		1988	
TAXABLE INCOME	MARGINAL RATE		TAXABLE INCOME	MARGINAL RATE
0–$1,800	11%		0–$17,850	15%
$1,800–$16,800	15%		$17,850–$43,150	28%
$16,800–$27,000	28%		$43,150–$100,480**	33%**
$27,000–$54,000	35%		Over $100,480**	28%
Over $54,000	38.5%			

* No 5-percent surcharge is in effect for the phase-out of the 15-percent bracket or personal exemptions in 1987.

** Taxable income between $43,150 and $89,560 is subject to a 5-percent surcharge reflecting the phase-out of the benefit the 15-percent tax bracket. A 5-percent surcharge is also applied to income between $89,560 and $100,480, reflecting the phase-out of the benefit of the personal exemption. The surcharges effectively make the top marginal rate on this income 33 percent. Once the personal exemption phase-out is completed, the marginal tax rate on additional taxable income drops back to 28 percent.

TAX RATES FOR MARRIED COUPLES FILING JOINTLY

1986

TAXABLE INCOME	MARGINAL RATE	TAXABLE INCOME	MARGINAL RATE
0–$3,670	0%	$32,270–$37,980	28%
$3,670–$5,940	11%	$37,980–$49,420	33%
$5,940–$8,200	12%	$49,420–$64,750	38%
$8,200–$12,840	14%	$64,750–$92,370	42%
$12,840–$17,270	16%	$92,370–$118,050	45%
$17,270–$21,800	18%	$118,050–$175,250	49%
$21,800–$26,550	22%	Over $175,250	50%
$26,550–$32,270	25%		

NOTE: 1986 tax-rate tables set by old law

1987*

TAXABLE INCOME	MARGINAL RATE
0–$3,000	11%
$3,000–$28,000	15%
$28,000–$45,000	28%
$45,000–$90,000	35%
Over $90,000	38.5%

1988

TAXABLE INCOME	MARGINAL RATE
0–$29,750	15%
$29,750–$71,900	28%
Over $71,900**	33%**
After phase-outs (e.g., income over $192,930 for a family of four)	28%

* No 5-percent surcharge is in effect for the phase-out of the 15-percent bracket or personal exemptions in 1987.

** Taxable income over $71,900 is subject to a 5-percent surcharge reflecting the phase-out of the benefit of the 15-percent tax bracket and personal exemptions. The surcharge effectively makes the top marginal rate on this income 33 percent. The phase-out of the 15-percent bracket is completed when taxable income reaches $149,250. Personal exemptions are then phased out; the income level at which this phase-out is completed will depend on the number of exemptions claimed. Once the personal exemption phase-out is completed, the marginal tax rate on additional taxable income drops back to 28 percent.

1986 TAX RATES FOR MARRIED PERSONS FILING SEPARATE RETURNS

1986

TAXABLE INCOME	MARGINAL RATE	TAXABLE INCOME	MARGINAL RATE
0–$1,835	0%	$16,135–$18,990	28%
$1,835–$2,970	11%	$18,990–$24,710	33%
$2,970–$4,100	12%	$24,710–$32,375	38%
$4,100–$6,420	14%	$32,375–$46,185	42%
$6,420–$8,635	16%	$46,185–$59,025	45%
$8,635–$10,900	18%	$59,025–$87,625	49%
$10,900–$13,275	22%	Over $87,625	50%
$13,275–$16,135	25%		

NOTE: 1986 tax-rate tables set by old law

1987*   1988

TAXABLE INCOME	MARGINAL RATE	TAXABLE INCOME	MARGINAL RATE
0–$1,500	11%	0–$14,875	15%
$1,500–$14,000	15%	$14,875–$35,950	28%
$14,000–$22,500	28%	$35,950–$113,300**	33%**
$22,500–$45,000	35%	Over $113,300**	33%**
Over $45,000	38.5%	After phase-outs*	28%

*No 5-percent surcharge is in effect for the phase-out of the 15-percent bracket or personal exemptions in 1987.

** Taxable income between $35,950 and $113,300 is subject to a 5-percent surcharge reflecting the phase-out of the benefit of the 15-percent tax bracket. The surcharge effectively makes the top marginal rate on this income 33 percent. The phase-out of the 15-percent bracket is completed when taxable income reaches $113,300. Personal exemptions are then phased out through another 5-percent surcharge; the income level at which this phase-out is completed will depend on the number of exemptions claimed. Once the personal exemption phase-out is completed, the marginal tax rate on additional taxable income drops back to 28 percent.

TAX RATES FOR UNMARRIED HEAD OF HOUSEHOLD

1986

TAXABLE INCOME	MARGINAL RATE	TAXABLE INCOME	MARGINAL RATE
0–$2,480	0%	$25,360–$31,080	28%
$2,480–$4,750	11%	$31,080–$36,800	32%
$4,750–$7,010	12%	$36,800–$48,240	35%
$7,010–$9,390	14%	$48,240–$65,390	42%
$9,390–$12,730	17%	$65,390–$88,270	45%
$12,730–$16,190	18%	$88,270–$116,870	48%
$16,190–$19,640	20%	Over $116,870	50%
$19,640–$25,360	24%		

NOTE: 1986 tax-rate tables set by old law

1987*

TAXABLE INCOME	MARGINAL RATE
0–$2,500	11%
$2,500–$23,000	15%
$23,000–$38,000	28%
$38,000–$80,000	35%
Over $80,000	38.5%

1988

TAXABLE INCOME	MARGINAL RATE
0–$23,900	15%
$23,901–$61,650	28%
Over $61,650**	33%**
After phase-outs (e.g., income over $145,630 for a family of two)	28%

* No 5-percent surcharge is in effect for the phase-out of the 15-percent bracket or personal exemptions in 1987.

** Taxable income over $61,650 is subject to a 5-percent surcharge reflecting the phase-out of the benefit of the 15-percent tax bracket and personal exemptions. The surcharge effectively makes the top marginal rate on this income 33 percent. The phase-out of the 15-percent bracket is completed when taxable income reaches $123,790. Personal exemptions are then phased out; the income level at which this phase-out is completed will depend on the number of exemptions claimed. Once the personal exemption phase-out is completed, the marginal tax rate on additional taxable income drops back to 28 percent.

Still a Progressive Tax System

At first glance, the new tax law might seem to abandon the long-held philosophy that the tax system should be "progressive" so that people of greater wealth pay a greater proportion of their income in taxes than those with lesser incomes. But despite the sharp drop in tax rates, tax experts believe the new system will be about as progressive as the old law. Rates tell only part of the story. Although the tax rates are sharply reduced by the new law, much more income will be subject to tax.

Even though many middle-income people will face the same top rate as millionaires, the wealthy still will end up paying a greater percentage of their income in taxes than the middle-class worker. How does that happen?

Some tax benefits that are available to middle-income taxpayers are phased out for wealthy taxpayers, including Individual Retirement Account deductions, personal exemptions, and the benefit of the 15-percent tax bracket. In addition, the new law curtails a number of tax breaks that have been used heavily by upper-income taxpayers in the past to sharply reduce their tax bills, such as tax losses and capital gains.

A Big Boost in the Personal Exemption

One of the major bonuses of the new law is the near-doubling of the personal exemption. This is especially good news for large families, and one reason why the new law is regarded as "pro-family."

The personal exemption rises from $1,080 in 1986, to $1,900 in 1987, $1,950 in 1988, and $2,000 in 1989. Beginning in 1990 the $2,000 exemption amount is increased to take account of inflation.

You get to claim a personal exemption for yourself, your spouse, and for each dependent. So a family of four would get to claim $7,600 in personal exemptions (4 x $1,900) in 1987, compared to $4,320 in 1986.

As previously explained, upper-income taxpayers lose the benefit of the personal exemption. Congressional tax writers, however, were not worried that the loss of the exemptions would have an "anti-family" impact on the wealthy. The feeling was that such benefits as the personal exemption have little influence on how large or small a family wealthier people decide to have.

PERSONAL EXEMPTIONS

YEAR	PERSONAL EXEMPTION*
1986	$1,080
1987	$1,900
1988	$1,950
1989	$2,000
1900	$2,000 indexed for inflation**

* Beginning in 1988, the benefit of the personal exemption is phased-out for taxpayers with taxable income over a certain level (i.e., $149,250 on a joint return, $89,560 for a single filer, and $123,790 for head of household). For instance, a married couple filing jointly with two children would lose the benefit of two of their four personal exemptions when their taxable income reached $171,090 in 1988. (They would lose the benefit of all four if their taxable income was $192,930.)

** Beginning in 1990, the personal exemption will increase above the $2,000 level to take account of inflation.

ELDERLY AND BLIND TAXPAYERS

Elderly and blind taxpayers will find they are no longer entitled to an extra personal exemption under the new law. Instead, they will receive an extra standard deduction amount, which will help non-itemizers, but not itemizers.

CHILDREN

Children who need to file their own tax return will no longer have the benefit of a personal exemption to help shield from taxes their earnings from savings accounts or part-time jobs. Under the new law, no personal exemption is allowed an individual who is eligible to be claimed as a dependent on another taxpayer's return. In other words, the parent gets to claim a personal exemption for each of his or her children, but none of the children get to claim a personal exemption on any tax return they may have to file. (See Chapter 12.)

Non-Itemizers Get a Much Larger Standard Deduction

For the great majority of taxpayers who do not itemize their deductions, the new tax law provides a big bonus: The standard deduction is sharply increased.

Not only will the increased standard deduction help people who have been non-itemizers for years, but millions of itemizers will find that claiming the new standard deduction is a better deal than itemizing. As a result, they will join the ranks of non-itemizers, who tend to have a much simpler life than itemizers around April 15. The Internal Revenue Service will also benefit, since agents spend a good deal of time and effort scrutinizing itemized deductions.

After full phase-in of the program in 1988, married couples filing jointly will see their standard deduction increased by 36 percent, and single filers will see a 21-percent increase. Congress gave unmarried heads of household an especially large increase of 77 percent. The standard deduction for single individuals and heads of household had long been the same. But recognizing the special financial burden of heads of household, lawmakers decided to sharply increase their deduction to make it closer to that of married couples filing jointly. Congressional tax writers felt that the costs of maintaining a household for unmarried parents were closer to that of a married couple than of single people without children.

Despite the increase in the standard deduction, you should still make the calculations to determine whether you are better off itemizing. Home owners and people who live in high-tax states often have enough itemized deductions to make itemizing worthwhile. You should especially make the calculation on your 1987 tax return, since the big increase in the standard deduction doesn't generally take effect until 1988. Only the elderly and blind get a big boost in the standard deduction in 1987.

STANDARD DEDUCTION

TYPE OF RETURN	STANDARD DEDUCTION		
	1986	1987	1988
Single	$2,480	$2,540	$3,000
Head of Household	$2,480	$2,540	$4,400
Married, Joint	$3,670	$3,760	$5,000
Married, Separate	$1,835	$1,880	$2,500

Elderly and Blind Taxpayers

People who are sixty-five or older or legally blind do not have to wait until 1988 for the big increase in the standard deduction. The higher amounts take effect for them in 1987. In addition, elderly and blind taxpayers get to claim an extra standard deduction of $750 for single individuals ($1,500 if the person is both elderly and blind) and $600 for each married person who is either elderly or blind. (If both spouses are sixty-five or older, the couple receives an extra $1,200. If both were elderly and blind, the couple would receive an extra $2,400.)

These extra deductions are in addition to the regular standard deduction of $5,000 for married couples filing jointly, $4,400 for heads of household, $3,000 for single individuals, and $2,500 for married persons filing separate returns.

For example, two spouses who are both sixty-five and filing jointly would get a $5,000 standard deduction, plus an extra $1,200 deduction for being elderly. That makes for a total standard deduction of $6,200. If only one was sixty-five or older, the total standard deduction would be $5,600.

A single elderly person will receive a total deduction of $3,750 ($3,000 standard deduction plus an extra $750 for being elderly). If this he was both elderly and blind, the total deduction would be $4,500.

The extra standard deduction is intended to substitute for the extra personal exemption that elderly and blind taxpayers received under the old law. The increase in the size of the standard personal exemption plus the extra standard deduction makes the new tax law a better deal for non-itemizers than the old law.

Consider, for example, a married couple, both sixty-five or older who do not itemize. Under the old law, this couple would have received a total of four personal exemptions. In 1986 that would amount to $4,320. Under the new law, this couple will receive only two personal exemptions but at an increased amount of $1,900 each in 1987, for a total of $3,800 for both. In addition, they would receive two extra $600 standard deduction amounts, or $1,200 total. Combining the personal exemptions and the extra standard deduction, they would receive $5,000 in 1987, $680 more than they received for being elderly under the old law in 1986.

Of course, the new arrangement is not as good a deal as if the couple could receive four personal exemptions at the increased levels. But it is still far better than under the old law, especially when you consider the increase in the base amount of the standard deduction.

For single taxpayers who do not itemize, the new law is also more beneficial. Instead of receiving two personal exemptions totaling $2,160 under the old law, they receive one increased exemption of $1,900 in 1987, plus an extra $750 standard deduction. That is $490 more than in 1986.

For itemizers, the story is different. Since they do not use the standard deduction and therefore get no benefit from the extra standard deduction, an elderly couple would receive only two personal exemptions totaling $3,900 in 1987. That is short of the $4,320 they would receive in 1986 under the old law from being able to claim four personal exemptions.

Beginning in 1989 all standard deduction amounts are indexed for inflation, including the extra amounts for elderly and blind taxpayers.

STANDARD DEDUCTIONS FOR ELDERLY OR BLIND TAXPAYERS

FILING STATUS	STANDARD DEDUCTION* 1987 and 1988
Single Elderly or Blind	$3,750
Head of Household Elderly or Blind	$5,150
Married (one spouse elderly or blind)	$5,600
Married (two elderly or blind spouses)	$6,200
Married, Separate Return, Elderly or Blind	$3,100

* Includes extra standard deduction of $750 available to single elderly or blind taxpayers and $600 for each married elderly or blind taxpayer. The extra deduction is doubled if the taxpayer is blind and elderly, i.e., $1,500 for a blind and elderly single taxpayer. A blind and elderly married spouse would receive an extra deduction of $1,200.

NOTE: All standard deduction amounts are indexed for inflation beginning in 1989.

The Mechanics of the New Standard Deduction

The standard deduction works a bit differently than it did under the old law for both non-itemizers and itemizers.

NON-ITEMIZERS: Under the old law, non-itemizers never had to deal directly with the standard deduction, because it was built right into the tax tables and tax rate schedules. If you take a look at the 1986 tax tables, you will find the standard deduction amount occupying the 0-percent tax bracket. On a joint return, for example, the first $3,670 of income—the standard deduction amount—is subject to 0 percent, or no tax. The 11-percent tax bracket does not begin until income exceeds that level. That is why the standard deduction under the old law was technically called the "zero-bracket amount."

Under the new law, the standard deduction will not be built into the tax tables. Instead, you will subtract the standard deduction amount from your adjusted gross income before you go to the tax tables. Then, the first dollar of taxable income will be taxed at the 15-percent rate.

ITEMIZERS: If you itemize your deductions, you will have one less calculation to make. You will no longer need to reduce your itemized deductions by the standard deduction amount. Under the old law, itemizers had to subtract the standard deduction so they did not gain a double benefit from the "zero-bracket amount" that was built into the tax tables.

Earned Income Credit for Low-Income Parents

One of the principal benefits of the new tax law for low-income parents is a sharply increased earned-income credit. The credit is a dollar-for-dollar offset against tax liability. If the credit is more than their tax liability, the taxpayer gets a rebate for the rest. After they file a return, they get a check in the mail from the IRS.

Beginning in 1987 the credit is increased to a maximum of $800, up from $550. Before taking effect, the $800 amount will be adjusted for inflation that occurred between 1984 and 1986. The credit will subsequently be adjusted each year for inflation.

The credit is gradually reduced for incomes above $6,500 in 1987 and above $9,000 in 1988. Under the old law, the credit was completely phased out by the time income reached $11,000. Under the new law, many more low-income families will be receiving at least a partial credit, since the phase-out will not be completed until income reaches $17,000 in 1988. These phase-out levels will also be adjusted for inflation.

The new law also requires employers to inform employees whose wages aren't subject to income-tax withholding that they may be eligible for the refundable credit.

Adjusting the Tax System for Inflation

The new law continues and expands the indexation of the tax system for inflation so that people do not have to pay tax on increases in income that merely keep up with the cost of living.

Since 1985 the tax brackets, the standard deduction, and personal exemption have been adjusted for inflation each year. The new law will adjust many more elements of the tax system for inflation, including the earned-income credit, many of the limits on contributions to pension plans, and the taxable income levels at which the benefit of the 15-percent tax bracket and the personal exemptions phase out.

Inflation adjustments to the principal elements of the tax system, however, won't begin right away. The income threshold for the 28-percent tax bracket and the standard deduction won't be indexed until 1989. Personal exemptions won't be indexed until 1990.

The twelve-month period for measuring inflation for the following calendar year's adjustment will end August 31 of each year, rather than September 30 under the old law.

6

PERSONAL DEDUCTIONS

Charitable Contributions

For generations the tax code has embodied the tenet: Give and you shall receive. The new law, however, is not quite as generous as its predecessor in rewarding taxpayers who give freely to charity.

Beginning in 1987 people who don't itemize their deductions won't be able to claim a charitable deduction. Itemizers will still be able to deduct their contributions, but the deductions will be worth less because of the lower tax rates. In addition, upper-income taxpayers who donate stock, artwork, real estate, or other appreciated property to museums, universities, or other charities may find the value of their deductions diluted by the alternative minimum tax.

Charitable organizations are worried that the reduced tax incentives will mean less giving. Congress is more hopeful. Lawmakers banked on the premise that people give from their heart because the charity is a worthy cause rather than in hopes of receiving a fat tax deduction from Uncle Sam. Indeed, people made generous donations to charity long before there was an income tax. And non-itemizers used to give freely before there was a deduction available for them in 1982. Furthermore, even after the top individual tax rate was cut from 70 percent to 50 percent in 1982, reducing the value of the charitable deduction, charitable donations increased. Finally, the new law's tax cut for individuals means people will be in a better position to give more to charity since they will have more disposable income. Whether the reduced tax incentives under the new law will affect the level of giving remains to be seen.

NON-ITEMIZER CHARITABLE DEDUCTION ELIMINATED

The non-itemizer charitable deduction passes into extinction only five years after it was first put in place by Congress. While the itemized deduction for charitable contributions has been around for decades, non-itemizers were not able to write off their contributions until 1982, albeit in limited amounts. The deduction was limited to $25 in each of the first two years and $75 in 1984. In 1985 half their contributions could be claimed. For 1986 100 percent of contributions are eligible for the non-itemizer deduction. Under the original timetable set back in 1981, when the deduction was enacted, the non-itemizer deduction was set to expire at the end of 1986. The new law did not extend it.

If you occasionally itemize deductions, you could take full advantage of the itemized charitable deduction by bunching your charitable contributions in a year when you expect to itemize.

ITEMIZED DEDUCTION REMAINS

Since 1917 the tax law has provided an itemized deduction for contributions of cash or property to qualified charitable organizations. Though the new law continues the deduction, it will be worth less. First of all, the lower tax rates reduce the value of the charitable deduction as well as all other deductions. People who used to save 40 or 50 cents in taxes for every dollar they donated to charity will now find themselves saving only 28 or 33 cents. Similarly, taxpayers who were in the 20-percent or 30-percent tax brackets will likely save only 15 cents on the dollar, instead of 20 or 30 cents.

The new law also makes deductions claimed for certain gifts of appreciated property partly subject to the alternative minimum tax. There is no rule of thumb as to who gets hit by the provision because of the many variables involved in determining whether one is subject to the minimum tax. But this change will likely affect only upper-income donors who make an especially large gift or who claim substantial amounts of other deductions relative to the size of their income. For everyone else, the deduction for gifts of appreciated property remains intact.

CONTRIBUTING PROPERTY TO CHARITY

Contributing artwork, stock, real estate, or other such assets that have appreciated in value has long been one of the most rewarding gifts that taxpayers can donate. The tax benefit is greater than giving cash.

The law allows you to claim a deduction for the full fair-market value of the property donated. In addition, you don't have to pay any tax on the property's increased value. Say you bought stock for $10 a share, and it rose to $100 a share. If you gave the stock to charity, you would be able to claim a charitable deduction for the $100 fair-market value. In addition, you wouldn't have to pay capital-gains taxes on the $90 profit. So everyone benefits. You avoid the tax, and the charity gets a bigger gift than if you had sold the stock first, paid the capital-gains tax, and gave the net proceeds to charity.

That treatment still applies under the new tax law. But you will have to watch how long you hold the property before giving it away to charity. If you don't hold it long enough, you could end up with a much smaller tax deduction.

Just like under the old law, capital-gains rules will continue to dictate the size of the deduction you are allowed to claim for gifts of appreciated property. Although the new law effectively abolishes capital gains for every other purpose, the rules will still govern charitable contributions of property. As under the old law, the new law will require appreciated property to be held more than six months in order for you to claim a charitable deduction for the fair-market value of the property. If the asset is held six months or less before it is donated, then the deduction is limited to the original cost, or "basis," of acquiring it.

For example, say you purchased stock for $10 a share, and the stock subsequently rose to $100 a share. If the stock were donated to charity more than six months after the stock was acquired, you're home free: You could claim a deduction for $100. But if the stock were donated within six months from acquisition, then your deduction would be limited to $10.

For assets acquired after 1987, the holding period is scheduled to increase from six months to one year. So if you acquire property in 1988 or thereafter, you'll have to hold on to it for more than a year before giving it away to charity in order to claim a deduction for the full fair-market value. (The increase in the capital-gains holding period to one year was mandated by the 1984 Tax Act, and the new tax law didn't alter that provision.)

THE ALTERNATIVE MINIMUM TAX AND THE CHARITABLE DEDUCTION

Upper-income taxpayers will also have to keep an eye on their overall tax situation when making large charitable gifts of appreciated property, because these deductions can become sharply diluted in value if the donor is subject to the alternative minimum tax. Only part of the deduction has to be added back to income when computing the minimum tax. That is the portion relating to the appreciation in value of the asset. For example, consider the above example of the $10 stock that rose in price to $100. The $90 gain is the amount that has to be included in the minimum tax computation. Congress rationalized making the $90 gain subject to the minimum tax as a way of preventing wealthy taxpayers from receiving a double tax benefit from the contribution—the $90 deduction plus being able to escape paying tax on the $90 gain.

Wealthy people who are vulnerable to the minimum tax may be able to safeguard their charitable deductions by making large contributions in years when they are not otherwise subject to the minimum tax. If you are making a large gift of tens of thousands of dollars, you would be well advised to seek professional tax advice, because proper timing of gifts can save substantial amounts in taxes.

GIVING AWAY OLD CLOTHING, FURNITURE, AND OTHER PROPERTY

If you are donating old clothing, furniture, or other property that has gone down in value since you purchased it, you need not worry about holding periods or the minimum tax. None of that applies in these cases. When you contribute property to such organizations as Goodwill Industries or the Salvation Army you can claim a charitable deduction for the fair-market value of the gift, which in the case of old clothing is typically only a fraction of the price you originally paid for it.

SEARCHING HARDER FOR ELIGIBLE CHARITABLE DONATIONS

With the value of charitable deductions cut back by the new law, you might want to search a bit harder to make sure you are claiming all the charitable deductions you are entitled to. In addition to the obvious cash donations to your church or synagogue, United Way, and the countless other charitable organizations, a wide range of contributions qualify for deductions.

Tickets to a benefit dinner, concert, or theater event qualify as charitable donations. The eligible amount is the difference between the normal admission price and the higher amount you paid for the charitable event. For example, if you paid $25 to attend a benefit motion picture premiere and the usual price of admission is $5, the amount eligible for the deduction would be $20.

Out-of-pocket expenses incurred in performing volunteer charity work are deductible, including telephone calls, uniforms, and transportation costs, which can be either the actual expense or a flat rate of 12 cents per mile plus parking and tolls. But the rental value of property you lent to a charity is not deductible. Nor is the value of your volunteer time, no matter how valuable it may be.

NEW RESTRICTIONS ON CHARITABLE TRAVEL DEDUCTIONS

People who were hoping to write off the cost of a vacation by performing a bit of charity work on the trip will be out of luck under the new law. The rules for claiming charitable deductions for unreimbursed out-of-pocket travel expenses have been tightened.

Congress decided to crack down after seeing a proliferation of tour programs that offered individuals the opportunity to deduct a trip to a nice vacation spot by performing some voluntary charity work while there. Tax writers found the charitable services performed were often minimal compared to the amount deducted, so they decided to deny deductions in cases where the travel involves a significant element of personal recreation or vacation.

The new law will still allow deductions for such expenses as the out-of-pocket costs incurred by a troop leader on a youth group camping trip. Just as under the old law, he would be able to deduct unreimbursed transportation expenses, as well as reasonable expenses for meals and lodging.

The new rules take effect beginning in 1987.

Medical Expenses (Itemized)

If you have medical bills that were not reimbursed by insurance, you may be disappointed by the new tax law. Beginning in 1987 the itemized deduction for medical expenses is scaled back, making it harder for people to qualify for any deduction and providing fewer benefits for those who do.

Out-of-pocket medical expenses will be deductible only to the extent that they exceed 7.5 percent of your adjusted gross income. That is up from 5 percent under the old law. What this means is that you will need hundreds or thousands of dollars of additional medical expenses under the new law before you are eligible to claim even a dollar in deductions.

If you have $40,000 of adjusted gross income, for example, you would be able to deduct only those medical expenses that exceed $3,000 ($40,000 x 7.5 percent), compared with $2,000 ($40,000 x 5 percent) under the old law. In other words, if out-of-pocket medical expenses in this example amounted to $3,001, all you would be able to deduct is $1, compared with a $1,001 deduction under the old law.

As you can see, you will need to have incurred a much larger amount in medical expenses under the new law to qualify for any deduction, and once you pass the threshold you will end up with a much smaller deduction than in the past. Furthermore, the value of any deductions claimed will be diminished because of the lower tax rates. And many more people will be claiming the standard deduction under the new law and thus will no longer be in a position to take advantage of the itemized deduction.

With all this in mind, if you have been counting on the tax deduction to help offset some of your out-of-pocket medical expenses, you should review your medical insurance policy to make sure you have adequate coverage in light of the reduced tax benefits. If you don't adjust the policy, make sure that you have adequate savings set aside for medical needs.

In some cases, working couples might be able to get a larger medical deduction by filing separate returns. Under most circumstances, filing separate returns will result in a higher tax than a joint return. But if the lower-earning spouse incurred large medical expenses during the year, you may be better off filing separately. The reason is that the deduction will be based on a lower adjusted gross income level and thus provide a larger medical deduction. You will have to calculate the tax each way to see whether filing separately will provide extra tax savings.

The tougher guidelines for the deduction will also make it necessary for you to rummage harder through your records in hopes of finding additional expenses that are eligible for the deduction. Of course, only medical expenses not reimbursed by insurance are eligible for the deduction.

In addition to the more common expenses, such as doctors' and dentists' bills and hospital care, exists a wide range of eligible outlays that is often overlooked. The list includes the cost of health insurance premiums, prescription medicines, transportation to and from your doctor's or dentist's office, birth-control pills, and special items such as eyeglasses, dentures, and hearing aids.

The deduction covers a broad spectrum of special medical services, including psychological analysis; plastic surgery; acupuncture; hair transplants; electrolysis; treatment for alcoholism or drug addiction; abortions; and the services of optometrists, opthalmologists, chiropractors, and podiatrists.

Prescription drugs and insulin are deductible medical expenses. But over-the-counter drugs do not qualify. Even if your doctor prescribes the drug, you will not be able to claim the expense if it is available on a nonprescription basis.

Health club dues and fees for stop-smoking clinics or weight-loss programs are not deductible if undertaken for the purpose of improving your general health. If the program is prescribed by a doctor for treatment of a specific ailment, however, the cost is deductible.

The cost of traveling to a specific locale on the advice of your doctor for relief of a specific chronic physical or mental ailment is deductible, although the costs of lodging and meals during the stay are not. For example, a person with a heart condition who is advised by his doctor that cold winter weather would aggravate his condition could deduct transportation expenses to Florida. But if you're not so afflicted with a specific ailment, a sojourn to Miami Beach in hopes of improving your general health and mental state is not a deductible expense, even if the doctor said it was a grand idea.

Getting to your doctor's office is a deductible expense. If you travel by bus, subway, or cab, simply jot down the fare. If you take your own car, you can either deduct the actual cost of gas and oil, or you can simplify your life and the paperwork burden by claiming 9 cents per mile. Parking and tolls can be also be deducted.

People who need to travel to a distant location for medical treatment, to the Mayo Clinic, for example, are allowed to deduct lodging costs of up to $50 a night per person, as well as transportation costs. For example, a parent traveling with a sick child can deduct up to $100 a night in lodging expenses.

Nursing home expenses are partly or fully deductible, depending on what the patient is there for. All costs, including meals and lodging, are deductible if the patient is in the home mainly to obtain medical care. If the patient is there for merely personal or family reasons, only the costs pertaining to medical or nursing care qualify for the deduction.

Even improvements made to your home on the advice of a doctor can qualify for a deduction, such as an elevator for a heart patient who has been warned not to climb stairs, or central air-conditioning for an asthmatic child. In figuring the deduction, you have to reduce the cost of the equipment by the amount the improvement increases the value of your home.

For a physically handicapped person, however, the new law makes the

51

full cost of certain improvements eligible for the medical deduction. This category includes expenditures incurred to accommodate a personal residence to the handicapped person's special needs, such as the construction of entrance ramps or widening of doorways to allow use of wheelchairs.

DEDUCTING EXPENSES FOR DEPENDENTS

In toting up your eligible medical expenses, make sure to include all the medical bills you paid on behalf of your dependents. Divorced or separated parents can claim deductions for medical expenses for a child regardless of which parent gets the dependency exemption.

ALTERNATIVES TO THE MEDICAL DEDUCTION

If you do not have enough expenses to qualify for the medical deduction, you still may be able to claim some medical-related expenses under two other provisions.

A few medical bills may qualify for deduction as an employee business expense, such as the out-of-pocket cost of an annual checkup required by your employer. But the options under this category are very limited.

Another alternative is the child- and dependent-care credit. If, say, you hired a nurse to care for an elderly dependent at home while you and your spouse were off at work, the expense could qualify for the credit.

Employee Business Expenses and Miscellaneous Itemized Deductions

Deductions for most types of employee business expenses and the category of "miscellaneous" itemized expenses will be sharply limited beginning in 1987. With few exceptions, both categories of expenses will be lumped together as an itemized deduction and made deductible only to the extent they exceed 2 percent of adjusted gross income.

The new limitation will affect a wide variety of expenses, including union dues, uniforms, subscriptions to professional publications, legal fees, tax preparation fees, investment expenses, the costs of hunting for a new job in the same line of work, home-office expenses, hobby losses, small tools required for work, and certain educational expenses to maintain or improve your work skills.

Only employee business expenses that were reimbursed, such as mileage allowance, by your employer will still be allowed as an "above-the-line" deduction that can be claimed by both non-itemizers and itemizers. These expenses will also be exempt from the 2-percent floor. All other employee business expenses, including those not reimbursed, will be allowed only as an itemized deduction and subject to the new 2-percent floor.

As a result of the tough limitations, most taxpayers will effectively lose the deduction. Most people simply don't have enough of these types of expenses to even get up to the 2-percent floor. After a while, many people will likely stop keeping track of these expenditures and forget about trying to claim the deduction. That will also help the Internal Revenue Service, which spends a good deal of time trying to audit and verify these deductions. The IRS has had frequent disputes with taxpayers over the guidelines for claiming such employee business and miscellaneous itemized deductions as home-office expenses, subscriptions to professional and investment publications, and safe-deposit box rental fees.

As for those people who do manage to come up with enough expenses to surpass the 2-percent floor, they will still end up with far fewer deductions.

For example, consider a person who has adjusted gross income of $40,000. For him, the 2-percent floor means his first $800 in employee business and miscellaneous expenses is not deductible. If he had a total of $1,000 in such expenses, he would be able to claim a deduction for only $200 ($1,000 − $800 = $200).

EMPLOYEE BUSINESS EXPENSES AND MISCELLANEOUS ITEMIZED DEDUCTIONS

HOW THE 2-PERCENT FLOOR LIMITS DEDUCTIONS

Adjusted Gross Income	Deduction Allowed to the Extent Expenses Exceed
$ 20,000	$ 400
$ 30,000	$ 600
$ 40,000	$ 800
$ 50,000	$1,000
$ 75,000	$1,500
$ 90,000	$1,800
$100,000	$2,000
$150,000	$3,000
$200,000	$4,000

For executives and other employees who have been paying a lot of work-related expenses out of their own pockets, the cutback in the deduction will mean that they will be bearing a larger share of the cost. With the federal government subsidizing fewer of these expenses, employees are going to be reluctant to foot as much of the bill.

"For a lot of executives, the new floor could well eliminate all the deductions they've got," said Herbert Paul, a New York tax attorney. "You are going to find a lot of executives renegotiating their employment arrangements to make sure all the expenses they incur get reimbursed, even if it means a lower salary."

EXCEPTIONS TO THE 2-PERCENT FLOOR

Aside from reimbursed employee business expenses, there are only a few exceptions to the 2-percent floor.

Handicapped employees are allowed to deduct their impairment-related work expenses in full without regard to the floor.

Gambling losses can also be deducted in full, subject to the usual limitation that losses are deductible only to the extent of gambling winnings. That means that if you spent $2,000 on lottery tickets and came up a $500 winner once, you would be able to deduct only $500 in gambling losses.

A few other arcane expenses are also exempt from the 2-percent floor, including amortizable bond premiums; certain costs of cooperative housing corporations; certain terminated annuity payments; deductions allowable in connection with personal property used in a short sale; certain adjustments where a taxpayer restores amounts held under a claim of right; and estate tax in the case of income in respect to a decedent.

PERFORMING ARTISTS

Struggling actors, musicians, entertainers, and other performing artists can, under certain circumstances, escape the 2-percent floor. Recognizing that performing artists tend to have especially large work-related expenses, such as agents' commissions, Congress decided to create a new "above-the-line" deduction for them that can be claimed by both itemizers and non-itemizers. The deduction will allow them to claim the business expenses in full.

Three criteria have to be met. First, the performing artist must have worked in the performing arts for at least two employers during the year. Second, allowable business expenses related to performing the artistic services must exceed 10 percent of wages from those services. Third, adjusted gross income, before deducting the expenses, cannot exceed $16,000.

Performing artists who don't meet the guidelines will be subject to the same 2-percent floor as everybody else. And only itemizers will be able to claim the deduction.

SELF-EMPLOYED

The 2-percent floor should not affect most people who have their own sideline business. If you have self-employment income, you can fully deduct expenses related to that activity by filing a Schedule C form.

Moving Expenses

The deduction for moving expenses, used by millions of Americans who relocate each year to take a new job or who are reassigned by their company to a different location, will not be subject to the 2-percent floor, but it will be available only to taxpayers who itemize their deductions beginning in 1987. The deduction was previously available to itemizers and non-itemizers alike.

Even for those still eligible to claim the deduction, its value will be diminished under the new law because of the reduced tax rates. As a result, if circumstances permit, you should try to negotiate a bigger moving allowance from your employer or future employer.

If you move, the deduction will still cover a variety of expenses that you personally have to bear and are not reimbursed by your employer. They include the cost of shipping your household goods; transportation, meals, and lodging while traveling to the new location; the cost of hunting for a new house before you move; and temporary living expenses at the new location while waiting to move into your new home or shopping for one. Some of the costs associated with selling your old home and getting a new one also qualify for a deduction, such as attorney's fees, escrow fees, and real-estate commissions.

There are no limits on the amount you can deduct for moving household goods and traveling to your new home. But the combined total of all your other moving expenses cannot be more than $3,000. Of that $3,000, no more than $1,500 can generally be deducted for house-hunting trip expenses and temporary living expenses.

The same rules for eligibility apply under the new law as under the old law, including the distance test, which requires that your new job location be at least thirty-five miles farther from your old home than your old job was.

Income Averaging

If you have a big jump in income, you will no longer be able to use the "income-averaging" method of calculating your tax liability to help ease the tax bite. The lower tax rates of the new law, however, should ease some of the pain.

Over the years, income averaging has been a big benefit for people who scored big in the stock market or the lottery, for employees who received a big raise or job promotion, or actors who moved from the unemployment line to a starring role. The income-averaging method effectively spread the income gain over a period of four years instead of just one year.

Income averaging helped prevent people who had sharp year-to-year swings in income or a rapid increase in earnings over a short period from being taxed more harshly than individuals who had relatively consistent earnings from year to year.

Congress felt that income averaging could be safely eliminated because with lower tax rates and fewer tax brackets people with fluctuating incomes would not be pushed into much higher tax brackets as frequently as under the old law with its steeply graduated rates.

Income averaging passes into extinction beginning with the 1987 tax year.

Political-Contributions Credit Abolished

Contributions to the campaign coffers of your favorite political candidates will no longer yield any tax benefit under the new law. The credit, which had been a part of the tax code since 1971, vanishes at the end of 1986.

Congress thought the political-contributions credit was a benefit that could safely be eliminated, since IRS statistics suggested that many of those who had been claiming the credit had high enough incomes to afford the donation without needing a tax subsidy. The credit, which had been claimed by a relatively small percentage of taxpayers, was limited to $50 for individuals and $100 on joint returns. (The credit was equal to half of the first $100 in contributions for individuals; $200 on joint returns.)

Presidential Campaign Checkoff

Although the political-contributions credit will pass into extinction, you will still find on tax return forms the familiar Presidential campaign check-off box. This box gives you an opportunity to allocate $1 ($2 on a joint return) of your federal tax dollars to the Presidential Election Campaign Fund, which helps finance the election campaigns of presidential and vice presidential candidates. Whether you check the box to allocate funds or not, the decision has no effect on your personal tax bill. The checkoff box neither increases nor decreases your tax liability; rather it is used merely to determine how much the federal government should provide to the campaign fund.

Nobels, Pulitzers, and Other Achievement Awards

If you were fortunate and talented enough to win a Nobel prize, a Pulitzer, or some other such meritorious achievement award, the federal government will now have reason to share in your joy. Beginning in 1987 these prizes and awards will no longer be tax-exempt. The only way to avoid paying taxes on the winnings is to turn the money over to charity.

Most prizes, whether they are won on a television quiz program or in a beauty contest, have long been taxable. An exception was made under the old law for certain prizes and awards that recognized achievements in religious, charitable, scientific, artistic, educational, literary, or civic fields. The best known of these awards were the Nobel and Pulitzer prizes and the Rockefeller Public Service Awards. But Congress thought that, in fairness, these prize winnings should be taxed just as are other prizes and wages.

Beginning in 1987 prize winnings will be taxable, unless you give the money to a qualified charitable organization. You will not be able to claim a charitable deduction for the donation, but you will avoid paying taxes on the award.

Unemployment Compensation

If you are out of work and receiving unemployment compensation, you might well end up paying more taxes under the new law. The reason is that unemployment benefits will be taxed just like wages. The limited exclusion for unemployment compensation will be abolished starting for payments received in 1987.

Congress decided to eliminate the exemption partly on grounds that unemployment benefits are essentially a wage replacement for workers who are involuntarily laid off, and therefore should be treated like wages for tax purposes. Lawmakers thought there was no reason that moderate-income workers should be taxed more heavily than unemployed persons with the same income.

They also saw that many recipients of unemployment compensation had income from other sources, or were married to a working spouse. In addition, there was some concern that because unemployment benefits were accorded favorable tax treatment, some individuals might have been discouraged from returning to work, where they might not earn much more after taxes than they received by staying home and living on unemployment benefits.

The increased personal exemption and standard deduction that the new law will provide individuals should help cushion the blow of having unemployment benefits taxed. But the fact is that many people subsisting on unemployment will have less to live on when the benefits become taxable. If you are caught in this bind, you will certainly have a stronger incentive to find a job quickly.

This change in tax treatment should also encourage all workers to set aside a larger pool of savings to help them in case they lose their jobs. This is especially important for actors and seasonal workers who predictably can expect to be frequently out of work and living on unemployment.

Under the old law, which still applies to payments received in 1986, no tax had to be paid on benefits for individuals whose adjusted gross income, plus their unemployment compensation benefits, did not exceed $12,000 ($18,000 on a joint return). Above those levels, part or all of the benefits were taxable.

Although unemployment compensation will become fully taxable, workers' compensation benefits will remain tax-free. This full exclusion applies to any payments under workers' compensation laws for personal injuries or sickness. Congress decided to make no change.

7

STATE AND LOCAL TAXES

Deduction for State and Local Taxes

The itemized deduction for state and local income, real estate, and personal property taxes remains fully intact under the new law. But beginning in 1987 sales taxes will no longer be deductible.

The loss of the sales-tax deduction will hit hardest people who live in states where sales taxes are a principal source of revenue. States with high sales taxes are likely to feel some pressure from residents to reduce their reliance on sales taxes because they are no longer deductible. As a result, some people may see proposals in their state legislatures to lower the sales-tax rate and increase income or property taxes, which will remain deductible.

States that have high income and property taxes, however, will not be home free. They will become relatively more expensive places to live, since the deduction for state and local taxes will be less valuable because of the lower federal tax rates. Thus, the real cost of paying state and local taxes will increase and state and local politicians will face greater resistance in the future if they try to raise tax rates.

But these effects are just the beginning of the story. The overhaul of the federal income tax system will have an immediate and profound impact on state and local finances and your state and local tax bill.

The Effect on State and Local Tax Bills

In more than thirty states, individuals will see their state and local income tax bills automatically go up because of the federal changes. The reason? These states tie their income tax to the federal system. Most of them use federal adjusted gross income or taxable income as a starting point on state income tax returns. The problem arises because federal adjusted gross income and taxable income go up under the new law. More types of income become subject to tax, albeit at lower rates. For instance, the repeal of the preferential treatment for capital gains means taxpayers will have to include more of their capital-gains profits in adjusted gross income. Under the old law, you were allowed to exclude 60 percent of your profits. Furthermore, in states where a deduction is allowed for federal taxes paid, the deduction will be smaller, since individuals will be paying an average 6 percent less in federal taxes under the new law.

So unless the states make changes to their own tax systems, many individuals will see their state and local tax bills rise, giving state and local treasury coffers a windfall from the new tax law. The National Association of State Budget Officers estimates that these increases in individual income tax revenues will range from 1 percent to 20 percent. In coming months one of the great political debates you can expect to see in state capitals will concern what to do with the windfall.

Officials in some states, among them New York and Ohio, have already vowed to return the windfall to taxpayers by lowering their rates or otherwise adjusting their tax systems. But not all states will. Some have expressed the need to keep all or part of the windfall to solve their own budget problems.

Four states—Nebraska, North Dakota, Rhode Island, and Vermont—have a different problem. They will collect less revenue under the new law because they base their tax systems on federal income tax liability. With federal tax bills going down an average 6 percent, these states will also see their tax revenues going down.

No effect on revenues is seen for Alaska, Florida, Nevada, New Hampshire, New Jersey, Pennsylvania, South Dakota, Tennessee, Texas, Washington, or Wyoming, according to the National Association of State Budget Officers. Most of these states have no individual income tax.

Additional Impact on States

State and local governments are also worried that other provisions in the new tax law will raise the cost of providing certain services. Many fear their borrowing costs will rise because the lower tax rates narrow the advantage of tax-exempt municipal bonds. Financial institutions also lose a tax break that had long made them major purchasers of municipal bonds. In addition, you may discover some services missing because of new restrictions on the type and amount of tax-exempt bonds that can be issued for certain purposes, such as low-rate home mortgages and student loans.

Calculating Your Combined Federal, State, and Local Tax Rate

Knowing your federal income tax bracket is not enough. State and local taxes, particularly in a high-tax state, can push you to much higher levels. Figuring your combined federal, state, and local income tax bracket will help you better assess how much deductions are really worth to you and the after-tax returns on investments.

Consider someone who was in the 50-percent federal income tax bracket under the old law and faced a 10-percent state income tax rate. Half of the state income tax rate would be subsidized by the federal income tax deduction. So this person effectively faced a combined federal, state, and local income tax bracket of 55 percent.

Now, if this person drops into the 28-percent federal bracket under the new law, only 2.8 percent of the 10-percent state tax rate would be offset by the federal deduction. That would make for a combined federal, state, and local tax rate of 35.2 percent.

8

INTEREST DEDUCTIONS

Personal-Interest Deduction Abolished

One of the most controversial provisions in the new tax reform law is the repeal of the itemized deduction for personal interest, which includes credit-card finance charges, car loans, student loans, and interest you pay to the IRS on overdue taxes. The category includes everything but mortgage interest, investment interest, business interest, and interest on deferred estate taxes.

The provision affects both new loans and outstanding loans—even those taken out long before tax reform became an issue on Capitol Hill. The elimination of the personal-interest deduction will hit hard people who have large outstanding debts, such as student loans.

The saving grace is that the personal-interest deduction doesn't completely vanish overnight. Beginning in 1987 the deduction is phased out over a four-year period, so that in the 1987 tax year 65 percent of your personal interest will still be deductible, 40 percent in 1988, 20 percent in 1989, and 10 percent in 1990. In 1991 no personal interest will be deductible.

For example, say you pay $3,000 a year in personal interest on a car loan, credit-card finance charges, a boat loan, and interest on late taxes to the IRS. On your 1986 tax return that is due April 15, 1987, you would be able to write off the full $3,000 as an itemized deduction. On your 1987 return, you will be able to write off only 65 percent of the interest, or $1,950. In 1988 40 percent, or $1,200, would be deductible; in 1989 20 percent, or $600; and in 1990 10 percent, or $300, would be deductible. In 1991 the deduction is completely gone.

Home owners have a way of circumventing some of the restrictions on personal interest deductions, which is detailed later in this chapter. Renters have no way of getting around the restriction.

PHASE-IN OF NEW INTEREST DEDUCTION LIMITATIONS

PERCENTAGE OF DISALLOWED CONSUMER AND INVESTMENT-INTEREST EXPENSE THAT CAN BE CLAIMED FOR DEDUCTION DURING PHASE-IN

Year	Percent Deductible
1987	65%
1988	40%
1989	20%
1990	10%
1991	0%

AN INCREASE IN THE REAL COST OF FINANCING CONSUMER PURCHASES

The loss of the deduction will raise the real cost of borrowing for consumer items, be it a car or a college education. In the past many people felt that with the interest deductible they could spend a bit more, perhaps getting a higher-priced model car or one with an extra option, since the federal government was subsidizing part of the cost. Now you will have to foot the entire bill on your own with no help from the federal government.

Certainly, the repeal of the deduction may well restrain consumer borrowing and spending and encourage people to pay their credit-card bills and taxes on time. Indeed that was Congress's intent in getting rid of the deduction. Congress felt the deduction encouraged people to borrow and spend rather than save and invest.

Economists, however, do not expect that everybody will suddenly stop borrowing money and saving much more. First, nearly two of three taxpayers couldn't deduct interest under the old system anyway because they didn't itemize their deductions. Second, many people pay off their credit-card bills before finance charges are imposed, and most of the others incur only a relatively small amount in finance charges each month. Third, some things simply can't be purchased easily without taking out a loan, such as a car and a college education. People buy cars because they need them, not because they get a tax deduction by financing them.

To be sure, the loss of the deduction is likely to have some effect. And the repeal of the personal-interest deduction is one reason why some economists believe the new law will help bring about lower interest rates.

To the extent the new law discourages borrowing and lowers interest rates, all taxpayers will benefit. And lower interest rates would help offset the loss of the interest deduction for those who itemize. The new tax law will also leave a majority of Americans with more money in their pockets to do with as they please because of the individual tax cuts. So, many economists predict that the tax law will stimulate consumer spending, rather than depress it.

Investment-Interest Deductions

Deductions for interest payments on money borrowed to finance investments, such as stock bought on margin, are also subject to new limitations, although they aren't as severe as those for personal interest.

Investment interest will be deductible only to the extent that you have income from investments, such as interest, dividends, or stock market profits. Thus, people who have large amounts of investment income will be able to deduct plenty of investment interest. If you don't have much investment income, you're out of luck.

For example, say you paid $2,000 in interest on a loan to buy stock and you had investment income totaling $1,200 from dividends and bank account interest. You would be able to deduct only $1,200 of the $2,000 in investment-interest expense. That means $800 of your $2,000 interest expense would not be deductible. But the $800 is not necessarily lost forever. You can carry the deductions forward and use them in a future year—subject to the new limitations that investment-interest deductions in any year cannot exceed investment income.

As with personal interest, Congress had mercy and gives some transition relief. In 1987 you will be able to deduct 65 percent of the disallowed interest, 40 percent in 1988, 20 percent in 1989, and 10 percent in 1990.

Using the example above, where $800 of the $2,000 is disallowed, you would be able to deduct in 1987 a total of $1,720 in investment interest ($1,200 plus 65 percent of the $800 in disallowed interest). In 1988 you could deduct $1,520, in 1989, $1,360, and in 1990 $1,280. In 1991 and thereafter the limitation becomes fully effective, and only $1,200 would be deductible.

In figuring investment income, you have to subtract investment expenses (other than interest) that you were able to claim as a deduction, such as investment advisory fees or safe-deposit box rental fees.

In addition, in figuring the amount of interest expense allowed during the phase-out period, you're still bound by the old law limits—i.e., investment interest is deductible to the extent of net investment income plus $10,000 ($5,000 for married persons filing separate returns). So if you had $20,000 in interest expense in excess of net investment income, only $6,500 of the excess (65 percent of $10,000) would be deductible in 1987 under the transition rules.

TAX-SHELTER INVESTORS

In tallying up your net investment income or interest expense, don't count any interest expense or income from tax shelters. But from 1987 through 1990 you will have to reduce investment income by the amount of disallowed tax-shelter losses that you are allowed to deduct during this phase-out period. Tax-shelter losses get phased out over four years just like excess investment interest. Assume that you had a $5,000 tax-shelter loss. In 1987 65 percent of it, or $3,250, would be deductible. Therefore, you would have to reduce your investment income in 1987 by $3,250 in figuring your investment-interest expense deduction.

Borrowing Against Your Home to Gain Deductions (Mortgage Interest)

For home owners the new law contains a loophole for getting around the new limitations on personal- and investment-interest deductions. Home-mortgage loans can be used to finance your purchases, and the interest paid on these loans will still be deductible. As a result, refinancings, second mortgages, and home-equity loans are likely to become even more popular borrowing options in the future.

But there are limits. Congress tightened up the mortgage-interest deduction so as not to leave too gaping a loophole.

Beginning in 1987 mortgage-interest deductions on first and second homes are limited to the sum of the following:

—The price you originally paid for the house.

—The cost of home improvements.

—Amounts borrowed against your home for qualified educational expenses.

—Amounts borrowed against your home for qualified medical expenses.

For example, say you originally paid $70,000 for a home and put $30,000 worth of improvements in it. Unless you were borrowing against your home for medical or educational expenses, you would be able to claim mortgage-interest deductions for up to $100,000 in loans secured against the house. (That $100,000 is the sum of the original purchase price and the cost of home improvements.) Now let's say that you paid your mortgage down to $40,000. That would leave you with room to borrow $60,000 against your house ($100,000 minus $40,000). The interest would remain deductible, and you could use the proceeds for whatever purpose you wanted—to consolidate debts, take a world cruise, or buy a sports car, a houseful of furniture, or a yacht. It doesn't matter as long as you are within the $100,000 limit.

If you had medical or educational expenses, you could borrow even more. Let's say you needed $2,000 for medical expenses and $20,000 to send a child to college. You could borrow up to $122,000 against your home and claim mortgage deductions for the full amount.

There's one other limitation, however. You can't claim deductions for borrowings in excess of the home's fair-market value. Financial institutions usually won't lend you more than the fair-market value anyway. But congressional tax writers didn't want to leave the door open for creative financing.

DEDUCTIONS FOR OLDER DEBTS PROTECTED

The new law protects deductions for mortgage debt incurred before August 17, 1986. That will safeguard millions of Americans who have borrowed heavily against their homes in recent years, pushing their mortgage debt beyond the new limitations. Many of them took advantage of the sharp appreciation in home values over the past decade to borrow extra money for a variety of purposes.

For example, say you bought a home some time back for $50,000 and it increased in value to $200,000. In 1985 you refinanced, enlarging the mortgage to $150,000. You would still be able to deduct interest on that $150,000 home loan, since it was incurred before August 17, 1986. From then on, you could increase your borrowing above the $150,000 (this amount gradually falls as you pay down your principal) only if you made additional home improvements or made additional borrowings against your house for medical expenses or educational expenses.

The IRS was expected to issue regulations soon that would address the question of whether refinancing the pre-August 17 mortgage debt would jeopardize the higher deduction limit (i.e., the $150,000 limit used in the above example). If it does jeopardize the limit, homeowners with large amounts of pre-August 17, 1986, mortgage debt could lose thousands of dollars in mortgage interest deductions if they were to pay off their existing mortgage and obtain a new one in a refinancing. As a result, you should wait for guidance from the IRS before proceeding.

QUALIFIED MEDICAL AND EDUCATIONAL EXPENSES

The kind of medical expenses and educational expenses that qualify for the home-loan deduction are briefly outlined in the congressional report accompanying the tax legislation.

Qualified medical expenses include amounts paid for the types of expenses eligible for the itemized medical deduction. The one exception listed is amounts paid for health insurance. Those payments don't count as a qualified medical expense for the mortgage deduction.

Qualified educational expenses include amounts paid for "reasonable" living expenses while away at school as well as tuition, fees, and course-required books, supplies, and equipment. Tuition expenses can be for primary or secondary school as well as for college or graduate-level education. The report stipulates that these expenses must be incurred within a "reasonable period of time before or after the debt is incurred." The IRS is also expected to spell out what "reasonable period" means.

HOW WILL THE IRS KNOW?

The question some might ask is: How will the IRS ever know my home loan was used for a car and not for medical or educational expenses? Indeed, these restrictions will not be easy for the IRS to enforce. But if you were audited, the IRS might ask for some records relating to the loan and when expenses were incurred. If you took out a $20,000 second mortgage two days before you purchased a $20,000 boat and five years before your child was old enough to go to college, the IRS agent would likely be more than a bit suspicious.

FINANCIAL INSTITUTIONS HEAVILY PROMOTING
HOME LOANS

Financial institutions have already begun promoting heavily second mortgages and home-equity loans in the wake of the new tax law. The advertisements tend to focus on how many dreams you can finance by tapping into the equity built up in your home. But you're going to have to keep an eye on the new deduction limits. Otherwise, you might end up with a loan that's not fully deductible.

The same applies to people who are refinancing their homes to take advantage of lower interest rates. Even if you don't intend to circumvent the restrictions on personal-interest deductions, you've got to be aware of the limits on mortgage-interest deductions. Otherwise you could end up not being able to deduct all of the interest payments.

Financial institutions will be looking at the fair-market value of your home in determining how much they are willing to lend you. But in terms of the mortgage-interest deduction, you will need to be focusing on other criteria. Keep in mind that the mortgage-deduction limitation is based on the original purchase price of the house—not the fair-market value—plus improvements and amounts borrowed for medical or educational expenses.

Rates on home loans are often much lower than unsecured personal loans. But you need to be cautious. Home loans usually entail "points," which often means paying an extra 2 percent or more of the loan balance as an upfront fee. You may also be stuck paying some closing costs as well.

Be aware that terms vary widely from institution to institution. In contrast to first mortgages, many adjustable-rate home-equity loans and second mortgages contain no limit on how high the rate can rise if interest-rate levels surge. Ask the financial institution for a disclosure document detailing the terms of the loan before you sign the papers.

Although a home-equity loan is technically a second mortgage, there are substantial differences between the two. With a second mortgage, you get a lump-sum check for the full loan amount when you sign the papers. By comparison, a home-equity loan is essentially a line of credit that you draw on as you need it, normally by writing a check but sometimes by the use of a credit card.

If you're buying a car, you may well find that home-loan rates are much higher than the subsidized financing offered by automobile manufacturers. Even if the interest is not deductible, manufacturer financing can, in many cases, prove the better deal.

One final word of caution: Keep in mind that if you default on home-loan payments, the lender has the legal right to foreclose, and you could lose your house. So make sure you're not borrowing more than you can safely handle.

9

HOME OWNERS AND RENTERS

Home-Owner Deductions

With home ownership long regarded as the American dream, Congress made sure to protect the sacred tax benefits available to people who own their own houses, co-ops, condominiums, and vacation homes.

The most valuable of these home-owner tax benefits, the itemized deduction for mortgage interest and real-estate taxes, were retained for principal residences and second homes. Only people with more than two homes will find themselves out of luck on the mortgage deduction for however many additional homes they may have.

Even though the mortgage-interest and property-tax deductions are still available, they will be less valuable to taxpayers than in the past because of the lower tax rates.

For example, consider a family that was in the 40-percent tax bracket under the old law and has mortgage-interest and property-tax payments of $1,000 a month. This family saved $400 a month in federal income taxes under the old law through the mortgage-interest and property-tax deductions. As a result, they had to pay only $600 a month out of pocket for the house. Under the new law, this family's marginal tax rate drops to 28 percent. That means the mortgage and property-tax deductions will save the family only $280 a month—instead of $400. Consequently, the family would effectively be paying $720 a month—rather than $600—out of pocket for the house.

As you can see, the new tax law will effectively be providing a smaller tax "subsidy" than in the past, forcing home owners to bear more of the costs. Do not be alarmed, however. You will not have to look far for the extra money to make up the difference because you will be saving a similar amount of taxes on income you earn. Instead of the family in the example above paying $400 in income taxes on every $1,000 of income they earned under the old law, they would be paying only $280 in taxes under the new law. That is a savings of $120, which will help them pay the additional $120 a month on housing costs.

Because of other provisions in the new law, many home owners will wind up with more money in their pockets, not less.

THE RELATIVE COST OF HOME OWNERSHIP INCREASES

If everything more than balances out, the question arises: What difference does it make if the mortgage-interest and property-tax deductions are not worth as much? The answer is that the relative cost of housing will go up as a proportion of the owner's after-tax income—even though his after-tax income might well increase. For example, a family that spent 30 percent of its after-tax income on housing might find it now consumes 37 percent of their budget under the new law. Some home owners wouldn't care. Others might decide that 37 percent of their after-tax income is too much to spend on housing. If they are shopping for a new home, they might well choose a lower-priced home as a result. Studies have found that people are sensitive to what percentage of their income goes toward housing.

How Property Values Might Be Affected

One effect of all this is to put downward pressure on property values. Housing analysts believe that the reduced tax benefits could depress home prices or keep them from increasing as fast as they otherwise might.

The biggest impact will likely be at the top end of the market, that is, high-priced homes that were purchased by people in the highest tax brackets. The reason is that these taxpayers will see the value of their tax benefits reduced the most. And this reduced tax "subsidy" is expected to translate into lower property values.

The impact on property values is expected to be much less in the middle- and lower-priced home categories because those buyers will not see their tax rate drop as far as those in the top brackets.

This decline will not necessarily occur overnight. More likely the impact will occur gradually over a period of years. Many home owners might not even notice the change, because property values might still rise. But they would fail to rise as fast they would have in the absence of the tax changes. The impact of the tax changes would be similar to the impact of an increase in mortgage rates of one to three percentage points.

Some analysts predict property value declines of as much as 10 percent to 20 percent for homes priced at over $150,000 in neighborhoods where the owners had been in the top brackets. Declines in the middle- and lower-priced home categories are projected to be 5 percent or less.

OFFSETTING FACTORS

Theoretically, home prices should adjust to the point where the after-tax cost is the same as it was before the law was changed. That is, a home that cost the owner $600 a month out of pocket after taking account of the tax savings would cost the owner $600 a month after taxes under the new law.

But for a number of reasons, the reduced value of the home-owner tax benefits may not get fully translated into lower property values. First, many people might view homes as one of the few tax shelters left and feel comfortable pouring more of their money into a home. Second, most people will have slightly more money in their pockets under the new law to spend on housing because of the projected tax cuts.

Third, people will find that their homes can be a valuable reservoir of extra interest deductions. Within limits, people can borrow against their homes to circumvent the tough limitations on other interest deductions. That is a loophole that renters will not have.

Furthermore, because of new limitations on consumer- and investment-interest deductions, many economists believe that the new tax law will help bring about lower interest rates.

FIRST-TIME HOME OWNERS

If mortgage rates drop, home buyers would be able to afford a more expensive home, and first-time home buyers would likely be drawn into the market, increasing the overall demand for homes.

Down the road, some renters who might face significant increases in their rents because of the new tax law might find home ownership a more attractive option. And because of the lower tax rates, many would-be home buyers will find it easier to save for a down payment on their first home.

Vacation Homes

Vacation homes will retain the same tax benefits as principal residences. People who own a seaside retreat, a house in the country, or a condo in a ski resort will be able to continue to claim deductions for mortgage interest and property taxes, making vacation homes one of the few surviving tax shelters.

As is the case with principal residences, however, these deductions will be worth less under the new law because of the lower tax rates. And that reduced federal government subsidy may matter more in the case of vacation homes than for primary residences. People need a place to live, but a weekend retreat is a luxury that people can live without.

A significant number of vacation home owners will figure the increased after-tax cost of owning a second home is a luxury they can no longer afford. Some people lucky enough to have more than one vacation home are likely to come to the same conclusion. For them, the extra home will be an extra costly luxury, since deductions for mortgage interest and property taxes will be allowed only on principal residences and second homes.

Further, many people who have been renting out their vacation homes and relying on the extra tax benefits to make the second home a worthwhile investment may also decide to abandon ship. Individuals with adjusted gross incomes under $100,000 will be able to claim up to $25,000 a year in tax losses generated by a rental property they own and look after. In most cases, that is much more than people claimed under the old law. But the value of those tax losses will be reduced under the new law by the lower tax rates. In addition, that $25,000 limit is reduced for people earning between $100,000 and $150,000. And those with adjusted gross incomes over $150,000 will not be allowed to claim any tax losses—meaning they would no longer be able to claim more deductions than the rent generated from their vacation home. The only salvation is a four-year phase-out period, which will ease the pain of the new rules. (In 1987 65 percent of disallowed losses can still be deducted, in 1988 40 percent, in 1989 20 percent, and in 1990 10 percent.)

All of these factors could have a depressing impact in some vacation home markets. Even before the new tax law was enacted, real-estate brokers in many popular resort areas reported a surge in the number of vacation homes put up for sale. Many more people were expected to try to unload second homes before the end of 1986 to take advantage of long-term capital-gains rates before they go up. The new law will tax profits from the sale of vacation homes at regular rates, just like other income. For 1987 the top rate will be capped at 28 percent for homes held longer than six months, even though other income will be taxed at rates as high as 38.5 percent for that year. After that, all gains will be taxed at regular rates.

Many real-estate experts believe that there will be some new buyers coming into the market, lured in part by the lower prices that many second homes have been fetching. After all, second homes will still offer tax benefits, in addition to the personal pleasure of having a private vacation hideaway. And they will also be a source of additional interest deductions. Second homes, like first homes, can be used to partly circumvent the new restrictions on consumer-interest deductions. In addition, the new tax cuts will give people a bit more money to spend on such pleasures.

Furthermore, if fewer vacation homes get built over the next few years because of the tax changes, existing homes may be worth more in the future and fetch higher rents, some housing analysts predict. That might at least make up for some of the reduced tax benefits.

In any event, if you are looking to buy a vacation home, you should make some calculations to see if the reduced tax benefits of the new law make the purchase affordable.

For people who use their vacation home partly for personal pleasure and partly for rental, the new tax law will force them to reevaluate whether they want the home to be considered a second home or a rental property.

A vacation home is considered a personal residence if personal use is more than fourteen days a year or 10 percent of the number of days it is rented out—whichever is greater. If you meet this guideline, the home will be considered a second home and you will be able to claim deductions for mortgage interest and property taxes. But the amount of rental expenses you can deduct, such as depreciation, will be restricted. Your deductions are limited to the amount of rental income generated.

If your personal use of the home is limited to fourteen days or 10 percent of the time it is rented, then your home will be considered a rental property, which means you may be able to claim rental expense deductions in excess of rental income—subject to the new $25,000 loss exception. The catch is that mortgage interest connected with your personal use of the vacation home will be considered non-deductible consumer interest under the new law, since the home qualifies as a rental property, not a second home.

Under the old law, mortgage interest could be written off regardless of whether the vacation home was classified as a residence or a rental property.

This change could make an especially big difference to upper-income vacation home owners with adjusted gross income of more than $150,000. They will not only lose the mortgage deduction but will also be barred from claiming rental losses. Thus, these owners may be better off spending enough time in their vacation home to ensure that it qualifies as a second home. By so doing, they will at least be assured of being able to deduct the mortgage interest, along with property taxes, for their personal use.

Selling Your Home

The favorable tax rules governing the sale of homes remain intact under the new law.

If you sell your home at a profit, you can defer paying any tax on the gain as long as you buy another home that costs at least as much as your old home sold for within two years. (If you are on active duty in the military service or if you work and live abroad, you have up to four years to buy a replacement home.) The tax is not eliminated but it can be deferred indefinitely—so long as you reinvest the profits in a new home each time you move.

Under this rule, the home you buy and the home you sell must qualify as your principal residence, not a vacation home.

If you buy a cheaper home than the one you sold, you will have to pay taxes on the profit. Your tax bill may be slightly higher under the new law because of the changes in capital-gains tax treatment.

If you are age fifty-five or older, you may be entitled to a onetime exclusion from tax of up to $125,000 of gain on the sale of a principal residence. (The exclusion is $62,500 if you are married and filing separate returns.) This exclusion can prove especially beneficial for elderly people who decide to sell their home and move into a smaller, less expensive home; move in with a relative; or move into a rental apartment. Under these circumstances, the deferral rules would not apply, but the onetime exclusion can shield part or all the profit from tax. In addition to meeting the age requirements, you must have owned and lived in the home for three of the five years prior to the sale of the home in order to qualify for the exclusion.

Residential Energy Credit Abolished

If you plan on winterizing your home, you will have to bear the entire cost yourself. There is no longer a tax credit available for home owners or renters who spend money on energy-conservation materials. Congress did not revive the residential energy credit that used to save people up to $300 in taxes for installing storm windows, insulation, or such other home energy-saving items. The credit expired at the end of 1985 and Congress decided not to reinstate it.

Just because the credit is gone, however, does not mean that the incentive for taking these measures is also gone. If you calculate your potential savings in utility bills, you will often find the savings exceed most expenditures you make on energy conservation.

Renewable Energy Tax Credit Eliminated

Home owners who have been toying with the idea of installing a solar heating system, a windmill, or some other such energy device will mourn the loss of an extremely valuable tax benefit—the residential renewable energy tax credit.

This credit provided considerable incentive to install home-energy devices that would tap the eternal resources of the sun, wind, or geothermal reaches to produce electricity or heat. The credit was worth up to 40 percent of the first $10,000 spent on such equipment, thus providing a tax savings of as much as $4,000.

Under the old law, the credit was set to expire at the end of 1985, and after some consideration, Congress ultimately decided not to revive it in the new law.

But as with the residential energy credit, you should not dismiss the idea of installing some energy-saving equipment just because the renewable energy credit has vanished. The savings on your monthly utility bills could well make such a device a profitable expenditure. It might also add to the value of your home.

Casualty and Theft Losses

If disaster strikes, and your home owner's insurance is not enough to cover the damage, some of the losses can still be written off on your tax return. However, you should look over your insurance policy to make sure that your coverage is adequate, because the deductions for casualty and theft losses will no longer be as valuable or as easy to obtain under the new law. In other words, you will not be able to rely on the federal government as much as in the past to be, in effect, a co-insurer of your losses.

The one direct change made by the new law denies deductions for amounts that would be covered by your insurance policy but for which you elected not to file a claim for reimbursement. The denial applies only to the extent the insurance policy would have provided reimbursement. The new law overrules some recent court decisions that allowed deductions for losses in cases where people had insurance but decided, for one reason or another, not to file an insurance claim. This change applies to losses sustained beginning in 1987.

The casualty deduction covers losses that are unreimbursed by insurance resulting from theft, vandalism, fire, floods, hurricanes, tornadoes, storms, and other natural disasters. Not all catastrophes qualify for the tax deduction, however. The Internal Revenue Service says that the disaster must be the result of an identifiable event that is "sudden, unexpected or unusual." This definition is intended to rule out deductions for damage caused by gradual or progressive forces, such as termite infestation. It is also meant to preclude commonplace accidents that occur under normal conditions, such as dropping glassware or china, or damage done to the living-room furniture by the family dog.

Losses resulting from an accident to your car do not qualify for the deduction if the accident was caused by your willful negligence.

The formula for figuring the deduction effectively limits the deduction to people who have suffered a loss of catastrophic proportions or those who have endured a string of lesser calamities. In figuring the deduction, you first subtract any insurance reimbursements from your losses. Then you subtract $100 for each loss. Finally, you reduce the total by 10 percent of your adjusted gross income.

For example, say you had a $10,000 loss and 60 percent of it was reimbursed by insurance. This leaves $4,000 eligible for the deduction. That amount first has to be reduced by $100, leaving $3,900. If your adjusted gross income is $30,000, you would have to reduce the $3,900 amount by $3,000 (10 percent of $30,000). Thus you would be able to claim a deduction for only $900 of your $4,000 unreimbursed loss.

This is the same formula under both the new and old laws. But the value of these deductions will be diminished under the new law because of the lower tax rates. Furthermore, many more people will end up using the standard deduction rather than itemizing, meaning that the itemized deduction for casualty and theft losses will be of no benefit to these people.

Finally, some taxpayers will see their adjusted gross income go up under the new law, since more income will be subject to tax. People with stock market profits, for instance, will see their adjusted gross income go up because they will no longer be able to exclude part of their long-term capital gains. If adjusted gross income goes up, you have to reduce your casualty losses by a larger amount in figuring your deductions.

Assume your adjusted gross income in the example above rose to $35,000 under the new law, from $30,000. Instead of reducing the $4,000 casualty loss by $100 and then by $3,000 (10 percent of $30,000 adjusted gross income), you would have to reduce it by $100 and then $3,500 (10 percent of $35,000 adjusted gross income). Thus you would be able to claim only $400 in deductions on your $4,000 unreimbursed loss, instead of $900 in deductions under the old law.

So with less help forthcoming from the federal government in offsetting your losses, you will have to look more to private insurance to protect your family from whatever calamities might occur.

Ministers and Military Personnel as Home Owners

Clergymen and armed forces personnel who receive tax-free housing allowances will be allowed to continue to claim deductions for mortgage interest and property taxes.

The new law effectively overturns a 1983 ruling by the Internal Revenue Service that precluded ministers from deducting mortgage interest and real-estate taxes on a residence to the extent the expenditures were allocable to a tax-free parsonage allowance received by the minister.

The IRS was considering a similar ruling for military personnel who receive tax-free subsistence, quarters, or other housing allowance. The new law puts that thought to rest. Military personnel are now assured that they will be able to deduct all their mortgage interest and property taxes.

The new provision is effective retroactively so that ministers affected by the original ruling can file for tax refunds, so long as the tax year is still within the statute of limitations.

Apartment Renters

One of the most worrisome side effects of the new tax law is the potential impact on apartment rents. Apartment dwellers could well see their rents rise more than they otherwise would in the years ahead. The reason: The new law sharply curtails real-estate tax benefits available to landlords and other investors in rental housing.

For years the tax code offered an abundant array of tax breaks to real-estate investors as a means of encouraging an adequate and affordable supply of rental housing in America. The tax benefits were so generous that investors were able to earn a profit on their apartment buildings even when tenant rents were not sufficient to cover the mortgage payments. With these tax benefits curtailed, landlords will attempt to raise rents in order to compensate.

"If there's one impact of the tax plan that's negative on lower- and middle-income taxpayers, it's the higher rent that they're going to be paying," said Kenneth T. Rosen, director of the Center for Real Estate and Urban Economics at the University of California at Berkeley and manager of real estate research at Salomon Brothers, the investment banking firm. Indeed, the rent increases could offset the tax savings that most taxpayers are projected to receive under the new law.

Apartment dwellers will not suddenly find their rents going up overnight, however. Landlords face significant obstacles in trying to raise rents quickly and sharply, either because of local market conditions or rent-control laws. If landlords were able to raise rents quickly, they would have already done so.

Rather, the increases are expected to come gradually over a period of several years.

The most immediate impact of the new law is expected to be a decline in the value of existing rental properties. If a landlord were to put his building up for sale, he would find that buyers are not willing to pay as much for the property as they would have paid under the old law. Buyers will pay less because the tax benefits are reduced.

At the same time, construction of new apartment buildings is likely to suffer a substantial decline as many investors shy away. At current rent levels, investors will find development projects only a marginally profitable or even a money-losing proposition.

Over time, this slowdown in construction will lead to a tighter housing supply in areas where demand is growing. Vacancy rates will drop, and landlords will find they have more prospective tenants looking for apartments than they have available. With demand outstripping supply, landlords will find that they can raise rents without weakening demand.

Theoretically, rents will rise enough to make up for the loss of the tax benefits and provide landlords with the same after-tax return as they received under the old law. This rise in rents, in turn, will reawaken interest among investors in constructing new apartment buildings and also push back up the value of existing buildings.

In markets where there is currently an oversupply of housing, such as Houston, the impact of the new tax law on rents might not be felt for several years. It will take years for the slowdown in construction to put upward pressure on rents, since so many apartments are already sitting vacant.

In areas where housing is already tight, such as Boston, the impact might be felt much sooner. In communities with rent-control laws, like New York City, landlords will face significant resistance in trying to increase rents quickly, even though housing supplies are already tight. Because of the threat of significant rent increases, some housing analysts predict that more communities will feel pressure to adopt rent-control ordinances.

Housing experts differ in their assessments of the size of the potential rent increases. But many of them predict that rents will rise gradually over a period of five to seven years to a level that is 10 percent to 20 percent above what they otherwise would be if the real-estate tax benefits were retained intact.

Some analysts predict that the impact on rents will be more moderate since the new law will bring about lower interest rates, thereby partly offsetting the curtailment of real-estate tax breaks. Furthermore, they think investors will continue to be attracted to rental housing because it still will offer some tax advantages, as well as steady income, along with real estate's long-standing draw as a hedge against inflation.

Should rent levels rise significantly, home ownership is likely to become a more attractive option for more people—particularly if mortgage rates decline. If you have been considering buying a home, this might be the time to make some calculations on the relative costs.

10

MARRIED COUPLES AND PARENTS

Working Couples—The Marriage Penalty Continues

Every April 15, many working married couples rediscover a costly fact of American life: The state of matrimony is no tax haven. The new tax law will do little to change this situation. For some people, the problem might even be exacerbated. For some others, the new tax law might provide a little relief.

Under both the new and old laws, the tax tables are designed in such a way that two-earner married couples generally pay a higher tax than they would as single taxpayers. This difference is what is commonly referred to as the "marriage penalty."

The marriage penalty does not arise where one spouse earns all or virtually all of the family's income. In fact, these married couples enjoy the most preferential tax treatment because the joint-return tax tables are the lowest of all of the filing categories. In the case of one-income couples, or where one spouse earns virtually all of the income, the institution of marriage can, indeed, be a tax haven.

The trouble develops when the second spouse's earnings provide a significant share of the family's income. That is because on a joint return the income of the second earner, in effect, is put directly on top of the first, so that the very first dollar of the second earner's income is taxed starting at high graduated rates. By contrast, the income of an unmarried second earner living with a companion and filing as a single individual is taxed starting at the lowest rates. In addition, two single individuals living together enjoy a combined standard deduction that is higher than the standard deduction available to married couples.

The marriage penalty generally becomes more severe as the couple's income rises and as the difference between the amounts the two spouses earned narrows.

To mitigate this marriage penalty, Congress in 1981 enacted a special deduction of up to $3,000 for two-earner couples. The deduction went a long way toward correcting the problem, but it did not eliminate the marriage penalty for many couples. The penalty still amounted to hundreds of dollars, and sometimes a few thousand dollars for higher-income couples.

Beginning in 1987 this two-earner deduction is repealed by the new law. Congress felt the deduction could safely be eliminated because the lower tax rates and wider tax brackets under the new tax system would minimize the marriage penalty. In addition, single individuals will get to retain more of their share of the standard deduction when they tie the knot at the altar in the future.

With the repeal of the two-earner deduction, the marriage penalty will be somewhat smaller in some instances and slightly higher in others. Some relatively high-income couples may see a larger increase in the marriage penalty.

You cannot escape the marriage penalty by divorcing at the end of every tax year and remarrying at the start of the new year. More than a few couples did just that until the IRS and the courts cracked down several years ago and largely curbed the trend. Nor can you generally escape the penalty by filing separate returns.

Marriage—To File Jointly or Separately?

In most cases, married couples filing separately will find their tax bill is higher than if they file a joint return. This is true under both the old and new tax laws.

Congressional tax writers closed most of the loopholes that might have made it profitable for married couples to file separately under the new law. For instance, a married couple whose income is above the threshold where the 15-percent tax bracket is phased out cannot escape the 5-percent surcharge by filing separately. Nor will married couples living together be able to circumvent the income-eligibility guidelines for Individual Retirement

81

Account deductions or the $25,000 in tax losses allowed for actively managed rental housing.

But there are a few situations in which it might pay to file separately under the new law.

One situation is when one spouse incurs large medical bills that were not reimbursed by insurance. If the expenses were associated with the lower-earning spouse, filing separately might produce a larger medical deduction because such expenses are deductible only to the extent that they exceed 7.5 percent of adjusted gross income. The same may apply if you had a large unreimbursed casualty or theft loss. Emil M. Sunley, director of tax analysis at the accounting firm of Deloitte Haskins & Sells and a former Treasury official, said another reason might be if one spouse incurs large employee business and "miscellaneous" itemized expenses, which will be deductible only to the extent they exceed 2 percent of adjusted gross income.

If you think you might benefit from filing separately, compute your tax for both joint and separate returns to see which produces the lowest tax.

Typically, the couples who file separate returns do so for reasons that have little to do with tax-saving strategies. One reason would be if the spouses, particularly in a second marriage, wish to keep their financial affairs separate and confidential and are willing to pay the extra tax to keep them that way, says Richard J. Stricof, a tax partner at the accounting firm of Seidman & Seidman. He said separate filing could also limit one spouse from being liable for the other's tax liability should trouble develop with the IRS.

Child- and Dependent-Care Credit

One valuable tax benefit left untouched by the new tax law is a credit available to working parents who need to hire someone to care for their child or a disabled dependent while they are off at work or looking for a job. Because this is a credit, which reduces taxes owed dollar-for-dollar, its value is not diminished by the lower tax rates under the new law.

The child- and dependent-care credit covers a wide range of expenses related to the care of a child under the age of fifteen or a physically or mentally incapacitated spouse or dependent of any age. The rules are liberal as to who can be hired, including a maid, a housekeeper, a baby-sitter, or a cook. Even payments to a mother-in-law or other relative count; even one that lives in the same house. The only stipulation is that the relative cannot be someone whom the parents claim as a dependent on their tax return. The law, however, draws the line at chauffeurs and gardeners. No matter how good they may be with kids, they are not eligible.

The credit has caught some unsuspecting people by surprise, since the compensation paid to household servants must be "on the books" in order to qualify for the credit. That means you have to comply with the rules regarding payment of employer Social Security tax (FICA) and federal unemployment tax (FUTA) on behalf of the household help.

The credit also covers some expenses outside the home, including day care, nursery school, boarding-school costs except for tuition, and even the cost of sending your kids to day camp or summer camp.

The credit applies to expenses of up to $2,400 for the care of one dependent; two or more dependents raises the total to $4,800. Eligible expenses, however, cannot exceed the lower-earning spouse's earned income. A spouse who is a full-time student is deemed to earn $200 a month, or $400 a month if care is for two or more dependents.

The credit is worth between 20 percent and 30 percent of eligible expenses, depending on the parents' income. Parents with adjusted gross incomes under $10,000 are eligible for a maximum credit of $720 for one dependent, or $1,440 for two or more dependents. For parents with incomes over $28,000, the maximum credit is $480, or $960 for two or more dependents.

Marriage and Divorce—Setting a Date

Timing can have substantial tax consequences on such basic decisions as marriage and divorce. This is just as true under the new law as under the old law.

A couple's marital status on December 31 determines their tax status for the entire year, and that can have a major impact on the year's tax bill.

While tax considerations should not be an overriding factor in deciding such personal matters as whether and when to get married or divorced, bear in mind that proper scheduling may save enough in taxes to pay for the cost of a honeymoon or the legal fees in a divorce.

One-income couples trying to pick a wedding date late in the year could well save hundreds or even thousands of dollars by marrying before year's end. The same is true for couples where one spouse earns virtually all of the income. The reason is that the tax tables for a married couple filing jointly are lower than those for single people with the same incomes. For the same reason, such couples should wait until the beginning of the following year to divorce.

On the other hand, two-earner couples earning about the same incomes should generally wait until the following year to marry—or divorce before year's end. The reason is the previously discussed "marriage penalty," where many two-earner married couples end up paying more than they would if they were able to file as two single individuals.

These are merely rules of thumb. If you are setting a date with tax savings in mind, calculate your tax liabilities both as single individuals and as a married couple before calling the caterers—or the lawyers.

Alimony and Child Support

The rules governing alimony do not change under the new law. Generally, individuals who are required to make alimony payments to a former spouse can deduct those payments. Recipients have to pay tax on those amounts.

By contrast, child-support payments are neither taxable to the recipient nor deductible by the payor.

The New Economics of Divorce Settlements

Even though the new tax law does not specifically address divorce matters, changes in the personal exemption, capital-gains tax treatment and the value of the deduction for alimony payments hold important implications for divorce settlements.

With the value of the alimony deduction diminished because of the lower individual tax rates, spouses are likely to resist paying as much alimony in future divorce settlements, since the after-tax cost of making the payments goes up.

Instead, the spouse will be more inclined to give away appreciated property, such as the family home, because of the repeal of capital-gains treatment. No tax has to be paid when the property is transferred, although the spouse who receives the property may encounter a big tax bill when it's ultimately sold. That is something the recipient spouse will have to take into account in the settlement.

With the personal exemption set to nearly double, some spouses will be eager to negotiate for the right to claim dependency exemptions. But wealthy spouses will likely be eager to trade them off, since upper-income taxpayers lose part or all of the benefit of the personal exemption beginning in 1988.

Deducting Adoption Expenses for Children with Special Needs

Families who adopt hard-to-place children will find the itemized deduction for certain adoption expenses is abolished in 1987. In its place the new law authorized the federal government to provide direct assistance for such expenses.

Under the old law, a deduction was allowed for up to $1,500 in expenses related to the adoption of a child with special needs. Eligible costs included attorney's fees, court costs, adoption fees, and other expenses directly related to the legal adoption of a child who is considered hard to place because of a handicap, age, ethnic background, or some other factor.

Authorization for the direct-funding program is provided under the Adoption Assistance Program (Title IV-E) of the Social Security Act. Ask the adoption agency you are dealing with for information on the reimbursement program.

Life Insurance Proceeds

Life insurance proceeds paid to a beneficiary on the death of the insured person remain tax-free under the new law. But a surviving spouse who receives the proceeds in yearly installments from the insurance company—rather than in a single lump-sum payment—loses a tax break. The old law allowed the spouse to receive tax-free the first $1,000 of interest included in the payment each year. Beginning in 1987 the interest exclusion will be repealed, but only for deaths occurring after October 22, 1986.

11

EXPENSE-ACCOUNT LIVING —BUSINESS TRAVEL AND ENTERTAINMENT

Write-offs for Business Meals and Entertainment

Writing off the cost of a night on the town or lunch at a posh restaurant as a business expense will still be permitted under the new tax law. But Congress decided that the federal government should no longer help foot the entire bill for such perquisites of corporate life. So beginning in 1987 only 80 percent of the costs related to wining, dining, and entertaining customers or clients can be deducted as a business expense. The 80-percent rule also applies when you dine out alone on a business trip.

THE IMPACT ON EMPLOYEES

If you are an employee working for a company, do not despair. The company is the one that loses 20 percent of the deductions for business meals and entertainment expenses. As before, your company should continue to reimburse you for the full 100 percent of your authorized expenses. The IRS will not make you give any of that reimbursement up. The only effect the new tax law may have on you personally is if the company decides to tighten its belt on expense accounts. In that event, you may find yourself wining, dining, and entertaining at less expensive spots, or doing less of it. But many companies consider such expenses as necessary and important to business as advertising. Thus, most companies are unlikely to cut way back even if 20 percent of the costs are no longer deductible.

THE IMPACT ON SELF-EMPLOYED WORKERS

If you run your own business, keep in mind that more of what you spend on business meals and entertainment will be coming out of your own pocket. The federal government will be picking up much less of the tab, not only because 20 percent of the costs will be non-deductible, but also because the value of these deductions will be diminished by the lower tax rates under the new law. Even so, entertaining and dining clients may still be a worthwhile expense given its value in building business relationships. In addition, part of the costs of your own meals and entertainment will still be subsidized by the federal government.

THE IMPACT ON EXECUTIVES AND SALESMEN WHO PAY THEIR OWN BILLS

Executives or outside salesmen who are not reimbursed directly by their employers for these expenses will find the write-offs for business meals and entertainment are further reduced by the new 2-percent floor on employee business expenses and miscellaneous itemized deductions. This will affect those executives and salesmen who are typically given a larger salary and then expected to pick up the tab for business entertainment and meals. If you have such an arrangement, you should consider renegotiating your salary or request direct reimbursement in light of the tax changes.

TICKETS—SCALPERS' FEES DO NOT QUALIFY

In addition to the 80-percent limit on deductions for entertainment expenses, the new law places special restrictions on tickets to entertainment events, be they to a concert, a play, or a sports event. Under the new rules only the face value of the ticket is eligible for a deduction. Fees paid to a ticket agent or a scalper no longer qualify.

For example, let's say a customer came to town and told you he'd love to see a particular hit show on Broadway. The only problem: The show has been sold out for months. Since this is a customer you are eager to please, you find a scalper who will sell you two front-row tickets for $150. Their face value is $50 each, or $100 for the pair. The other $50 represents the scalper's "handling fee." Under the new tax law only the $100 face value of the tickets would qualify for the deduction, and only 80 percent of that amount would be deductible. In other words, you would end up with a deduction of only $80 (80 percent x $100 face value) even though you paid a total of $150 for the tickets.

Banquet Meeting Exceptions

Exempt from the 80-percent restriction on meal expenses are certain banquets where a speaker is featured. Since many politicians speak at banquets, particularly in election years, Congress made an exception for 1987 and 1988—long enough to take them through the 1988 election campaigns.

The banquet has to be part of a convention, seminar, annual meeting, or similar business meeting and include a speaker. In addition, more than half of the participants have to be away from home, and at least forty people have to attend the banquet.

Charitable Sports Events Exempt

Tickets and related expenses at certain charitable sports events are exempt from the 80-percent business entertainment limitation. To qualify, all of the net proceeds from the event have to be contributed to the charitable organization. And volunteers have to be used for substantially all the work performed in carrying out the event, although paid concessionaires and security personnel can be hired.

Congressional tax writers indicated that tickets to college or high-school football or basketball games generally do not qualify for the exception, since the schools usually pay the coaches for their services.

Stadium Skybox Write-off Eliminated

Another restriction on entertainment expenses applies to skyboxes at amphitheaters and sports stadiums where corporate executives can watch athletic encounters in luxurious splendor. Write-offs for the extra expense of leasing these plush spectators' quarters for more than one event come to an end after a two-year phase-out. While Congress was willing to continue allowing entertainment deductions for the cost of regular stadium seats, lawmakers felt that the federal government should no longer be subsidizing the cost of skyboxes, which often rent for $50,000 a year.

The loss of the deduction will make skyboxes a much more expensive corporate luxury. Nevertheless, after entertaining clients in the comfort and prestigious environs of skyboxes, which often come complete with such accoutrements as TVs, restrooms, food service, and bars, many companies will be more than a bit reluctant to take their customers back to the regular stadium seats where the huddled masses sit. Even if the loss of the deduction forces some companies to move, it is unlikely that many skyboxes will stand empty for long. There are long waiting lists for skyboxes at many stadiums.

Companies will have a couple of years to adjust. One third of the deductions will disappear in 1987, and two thirds in 1988. After that, the only costs that will still be eligible for a deduction are food and beverage bills and the equivalent cost of regular box seat tickets for each seat in a skybox.

Extra Ground Rules for Meal and Entertainment Expenses

Congress and the IRS have long recognized the potential for abuse in the area of business meals and entertainment deductions. As a result, both the old and new laws require that such expenditures be ordinary and necessary to the active conduct of business and that it be either "directly related to" or "associated with" the active conduct of business.

The rules do not require you to spend the entire hockey game trying to convince your guest to buy a truckload of your company's widgets. But you would generally be required to hold a substantial and bona fide business discussion with the customer before or after the entertainment event.

Wining and dining have long been subject to less stringent rules. An executive could take a potential customer to a restaurant for dinner or to a bar for cocktails, and the expense would have qualified for a deduction even if not a word of business was uttered before, during, or after the meal. The one requirement was that the setting be conducive to a business discussion. That means no floor shows or other distractions.

But the new law tightens up on business meals by requiring that business has to be discussed during or directly before or after the meal. (Obviously, the rule does not apply when you are dining out alone on a business trip.)

The new law also repeats the long-standing warning that meal expenditures cannot be "lavish or extravagant under the circumstances" to qualify for the deduction.

Traveling on Business via Ocean Liner

Just about the time *The Love Boat* was canceled as a weekly television series, congressional tax writers decided to crack down on businesspeople who prefer ocean liners to the more conventional modes of transportation for business trips.

If you have business to attend to in London and you want to take the *QE2* rather than fly over, you will still be able to claim some deductions. But you may not be able to write off the entire cost. The new law places strict limits on the amount of the cruise fare that can be written off as a business expense.

Generally, such deductions are limited to twice the highest amount that federal government employees working in the executive branch are allowed for travel. The latest federal per-diem allowance was $126. Thus, the deductions for a business trip by ocean liner would be limited to $252 a day, or $1,764 for a seven-day cruise.

Congress suspected that many people who chose to travel by ocean liner on business were doing so for personal enjoyment. Otherwise, the lawmakers reasoned, they would have used another mode of travel that was faster and normally cheaper, and thus more appropriate for business purposes.

The change, which is effective beginning in 1987, does not alter the rules regarding conventions held aboard cruise ships. These rules, which were not changed by the new law, limit deductions for cruise-ship conventions to $2,000 per taxpayer per year and restricts the deductions to ships registered in the United States that stop only at ports of call in this country or its possessions. If not, no deductions are allowed.

Investment-Seminars Deduction Repealed

If you plan to attend an investment seminar, perhaps one in a tropical resort area where you can combine a vacation and a little advice on investment strategy, do not count on the federal government to help subsidize the trip. These deductions are abolished under the new tax law.

In recent years, investment seminars became a popular way to take a tax-deductible trip to Florida, California, Hawaii, or other vacation spots. Even if the main attraction was a chance to hear some renowned investment advisers speak on stocks, real estate, tax shelters, gold, commodities, and the like, the drawing card for many people was the added opportunity to spend a few days in some nice vacation spot and write off the trip on their tax return as an investment expense. These seminar programs were often structured so as to allow plenty of leisure time for those who attended. The

IRS tried cracking down on these deductions, but the revenue service was not able to completely abolish them.

The new law makes it very clear. Beginning in 1987 these deductions go out the window. And with them may go many of these investment seminars. If you want to attend one, keep in mind that you will be footing the entire bill with no help from Uncle Sam.

Teachers and Trips for Educational Pursuit

Teachers who are accustomed to writing off their trips to Europe and other far-off spots as an educational expense may be disappointed with the new tax law. With few exceptions, those trips will no longer be deductible.

Under the old law taxpayers were able to deduct the cost of a trip as an educational expense if the sojourn was to "maintain or improve skills" required in their work. Most commonly, teachers took advantage of this provision to make tax-deductible trips during school vacation periods or while on sabbatical leave.

For example, a French-language teacher who traveled to France to brush up on her accent was allowed to deduct the cost of the trip as an educational expense even though most of her itinerary might have included such pleasurable activities as attending movies, lectures, and plays, and visiting with French families. Similarly, a management professor who spent his sabbatical touring factories across Europe could write off the cost of the trip.

Congressional tax writers thought that this deduction was unfair in that it allowed some individuals in particular professions to deduct the cost of a vacation trip, while most people have to pay for their pleasure travels out of their after-tax dollars, no matter how educationally stimulating the trip. So Congress decided to ban deductions for travel costs that would be deductible only on the ground that the travel itself constitutes a form of education.

Beginning in 1987 deductions will be available only under very limited circumstances—such as engaging in research that can be performed only at a particular facility. One example cited to demonstrate Congress's intent is a scholar of French literature who travels to Paris to do specific library research that cannot be done anywhere else. Another example is someone who needs to take courses that are offered only at the Sorbonne.

12

CHILDREN AND STUDENTS

Children and Taxes: An Overview

For children with income, be it from an after-school job or a bank account in their name, a bit more tax may have to be paid under the new law. Children lose a number of advantages they used to have.

Parents will still be able to put money in a child's savings account and have the interest taxed at the child's lower rates. But for children under age fourteen, Congress decided to limit this benefit to the first $1,000 a year in investment income. Anything in excess of $1,000 a year gets taxed at the parents' rates.

In addition, children lose the benefit of a personal exemption to help shield some of their income from tax. For most younger children, only the first $500 of investment income will be free from tax, less than half of what the old law allowed.

The changes take effect in 1987 and apply to both new and previously existing children's accounts. There is no protection for those who saved up before.

Children's Bank Accounts and Other Investment Income

Congress found that parents were giving their children large amounts of money, stocks, and other income-producing assets. In the child's custodial account, income from these assets would be taxed at the child's rates rather than at the parents' rates. Since the child usually had little, if any, other income, the child would be in a very low tax bracket and would end up paying little or no tax. Hardly a better tax shelter existed. Money simply could be shifted from parent to child, and hundreds or thousands of dollars in tax savings would be realized.

Certainly, most parents didn't view it as a tax shelter scheme. They were putting nominal amounts of money away into a child's account for the purpose of saving for his or her college education and using the tax savings to build a larger nest egg. Congress thought that was fine. But they didn't want to allow parents to be able to shift large amounts of money to their younger children's accounts in order to shelter the family's income from taxes.

So tax writers set some new guidelines. One set of rules affects children under age fourteen. Another applies to accounts of children fourteen or over.

For children under age fourteen, the first $1,000 a year of their investment income will be taxed at their own low rates, just like before. That would effectively protect a child's account that had up to $12,500 in savings in it (assuming it had earned 8 percent interest). Investment income in excess of $1,000 a year, however, would be taxed at the parents' rates. (If the parents are divorced, the tax rate of the parent who has custody of the child would be used in figuring the tax.) So if a child's custodial account earned $2,300 in interest for the year, the first $1,000 would be taxed at the child's rate, and the next $1,300 would be taxed at the parents' rate. If both the child and the parent were in the 15-percent tax brackets, the change in rules wouldn't matter.

Nor does it matter who gives the money to the child. Whether it is the parent, an uncle, a grandfather, or a family friend, the money is taxed the same.

For children age fourteen or older, Congress decided to allow all the child's income to still be taxed at the child's own rates.

But that's not the end of the story. Children—no matter what their age—won't be able to claim a personal exemption as they did in the past to shield some of their income from the tax collector. Under the old law, the first $1,080 in income earned would escape tax because of the personal exemption. Under the new law, children will be able to use up to $500 of their standard deduction to shield their investment income from tax. (Under the old law, the standard deduction could be used only to offset income from a job.) So only $500 of their investment income will escape tax beginning in 1987.

For example, if a child under fourteen had $1,200 in investment income, the first $500 would be shielded from tax by the standard deduction. The next $500 would be taxed at his own 15-percent rate. And the final $200 would be taxed at his parents' rate.

If the child was fourteen or older, the first $500 would be shielded from tax by the standard deduction. And the rest of the money would be taxed at his or her own tax rate of 15 percent.

These threshold amounts are all to be adjusted for inflation each year beginning in 1989.

Children's Trusts

For children of any age, the tax law dealt a death blow to Clifford Trusts, spousal-remainder trusts, and other such "grantor" trust arrangements that were becoming extremely popular ways for parents to shift income to a child and save on taxes without losing title to their investment holdings. "You can say that Clifford Trusts have been repealed for all intents and purposes," said Thomas W. Kuchta, a tax partner at the accounting firm Price Waterhouse.

These trusts were popular because the parent could put stocks or other income-producing assets in the trust, have the income taxed to the child, and then take the property back after ten years. As a result, there was no worry that the child would end up with the legal right to the fortune and use it to buy a sports car instead of paying for college expenses.

Congress thought that these trust arrangements were merely gimmicks that allowed parents to cut their tax bills by filling trusts with income-producing assets that they would eventually get back. So tax writers decided to effectively kill off the trusts by taxing the income to the grantor, which is typically the parent, rather than to the child.

The new tax treatment will apply to trusts established after March 1, 1986. As a result, trusts established on or before March 1, 1986, are protected from the new rules, with two exceptions. Income-producing property transferred to existing trusts after March 1, 1986, are not exempt from the new rules, so there is no benefit to be gained by putting anything more in existing trusts. In addition, trust income distributed to the account of a child under age fourteen falls under the new rules relating to investment income of younger children, i.e., amounts in excess of $1,000 will be taxed at the parents' rates.

Taxing Income from a Summer or After-School Job

Children who earn money from a summer job or after-school job will benefit from an increased standard deduction, just like adults. In 1987 the standard deduction will help shield the first $2,540 in job income from taxes, and in 1988 the first $3,000. But as with investment income, they will no longer be able to claim a personal exemption of their own to help shield even more of their income from taxes.

Nonetheless, income from a job is always taxed at the child's rate, no matter what the child's age. Only investment income gets treated differently for children under fourteen.

The tax treatment gets a bit complicated when children have income both from a job (which is technically called "earned income") and from investments (referred to as "unearned income"). Simply put, the standard deduction the child can claim is generally limited to the amount earned on the job or $500, whichever is greater. For example, consider a child who earns $800 from mowing lawns and $900 interest from a bank account. The child gets to claim a standard deduction of $800.

When a Child Has to File a Tax Return

Under the new law children will need to file a tax return only when their income exceeds the amount of the standard deduction they are allowed to claim. For a child with investment income only, a return would not have to be filed unless income exceeded $500.

New Strategies

With the change in tax rules for younger children, the question arises as to whether parents should simply hold off giving any money to a child until the child turns fourteen. Certainly, the advantages are not as great as they were when the income was all taxed to the child, and the difference between the child's tax bracket and the parents' was much sharper.

But there still are benefits. For parents in a higher tax bracket, the first $1,000 of investment income earned in a younger child's account each year is still treated favorably. And once the child turns fourteen, all the investment income from the built-up nest egg will be taxed at the child's rate.

But tax advisers have been trying to think of some new strategies. High-yielding investments were traditionally recommended for children's accounts because the income was partly or fully sheltered. They may still be the preferred choice for children over age fourteen as well as for children under fourteen who have less than $1,000 a year of investment income.

For children under fourteen with larger amounts of investment income, new strategies are being devised. Instead of investments that generate taxable income each year, tax advisers say, parents should consider investments that defer taxable income until the child reaches age fourteen, when the income will be taxed at the lowest rate.

If the child is very close to fourteen—say, thirteen years old—the answer might be as simple as a one-year Treasury bill that does not mature until the child reaches age fourteen, said David S. Rhine, a tax partner at the accounting firm Seidman & Seidman.

For younger children, many advisers are suggesting that parents who want to transfer larger sums to their younger children might consider U.S. Savings Bonds, where taxes on the interest can be deferred until the bond matures. By that time, the child would presumably be at least fourteen years old, and the proceeds would be taxed at the child's rates. (See "U.S. Savings Bonds" in Chapter 15.)

Other tax advisers are suggesting that some parents might be better off simply investing in municipal bonds instead of transferring money to the younger child. You should make some calculations first to see if there is an advantage. The benefit will vary from individual to individual. Zero-coupon bonds, which sell for a fraction of their ultimate redemption value, are no longer as attractive as they used to be for a younger child's account. These bonds pay no interest each year, but you still have to pay taxes each year on what would theoretically have been paid to you. These were attractive as investments for children's accounts, since the child was in a low enough tax bracket that little if any taxes had to be paid. With the tax treatment changed, some investment dealers have been promoting tax-exempt zero-coupon bonds as the new alternative.

Even with the tax changes, wealthy parents may still wish to transfer larger sums to their younger children to save on estate taxes. Each parent can transfer $10,000 a year to a child (a couple can give a total of $20,000 a year to each child) without incurring a gift tax.

As for parents who are reluctant to transfer large amounts out of concern that the child will have the legal right to do anything with the money he or she wants upon reaching majority age, Mr. Rhine said trust arrangements can be made that will "protect the money from the child and the child from the money."

Scholarships, Fellowships, and Student Loans

Students and their parents will undoubtedly be unhappy to find that the tax-free status of scholarships and fellowships has been eroded by the new law. Some scholarship income will still be exempt for students seeking degrees. But non-degree candidates will lose the limited exemption they had under the old law.

STUDENTS SEEKING DEGREES

For students seeking degrees, the tax-free status of scholarships and fellowships still applies to amounts required for tuition and course-required fees, books, supplies, and equipment. But additional amounts, such as for room, board, or incidental expenses, become subject to tax under the new law.

The tax exemption is also abolished for any portion received as a grant or tuition reduction that represents payment for teaching, research, or other services required as a condition of receiving the grant. The tax exemption is also lost for federal grants where the student is required to perform future services as a federal employee.

NON-DEGREE CANDIDATES

The new law does away with the limited exclusion that was available under the old law for non-degree candidates. The old law allowed an exclusion of up to $300 a month for up to thirty-six months.

PROTECTIONS FOR PREVIOUSLY GRANTED SCHOLARSHIPS

The new provisions apply only to scholarships and fellowships granted on or after August 17, 1986. These scholarships and fellowships generally won't start being taxed until 1987. The old law applies for amounts received in 1986 that are attributable to expenses incurred in 1986.

Students who receive money from scholarships and fellowships granted before August 17, 1986, don't have to worry about the new rules.

HOW SCHOLARSHIPS ARE TAXED

The portion of scholarship or fellowship income that is subject to tax is considered "earned income," so students can use their standard deduction to help shield part or all of the income from tax. The first $3,000 in income will escape tax in 1988 when the standard deduction for single individuals increases to $3,000. For example, consider a student who received $5,000 in scholarship income that was not eligible for the tax exclusion. If he had no other income, the first $3,000 of the scholarship would be shielded by the standard deduction. The other $2,000 would be taxed at 15 percent, for a total tax bill of $300.

Only students who aren't eligible to be claimed as dependents on their parents' returns will be able to use the personal exemption in addition to the standard deduction to help shield the scholarship income from tax.

STUDENT LOANS NO LONGER DEDUCTIBLE

The repeal of the consumer-interest deduction will also increase the real cost of financing a college education because college loans fall into the category of consumer loans. Home owners will be able to get around the restriction by borrowing against their home. Home loans will still be deductible for educational purposes. But before you borrow against your home you should check other financing sources. Low-rate student loans, even though they won't be deductible, may still end up being cheaper than borrowing against your house. Shop around and check the terms. Renters have no choice. They have no way to circumvent the new restrictions on the consumer-interest deduction.

REEXAMINING YOUR FUTURE NEEDS

Students and parents will need to take these tax changes into account in calculating their financial needs for college. These changes may require saving more, borrowing more, working a summer job, or taking an after-school job. Nevertheless, given the cost of college these days, the extra tax burden is relatively small compared to the amount that is needed to send a child to school.

To be sure, many parents will have a tougher time saving for a child's college education without the full tax benefits of custodial accounts and the elimination of Clifford Trusts. But the lower tax rates should cushion some of the blow.

COLLEGES HIT BY OTHER WOES

Colleges and universities will not have an easy time dealing with the tax changes either. Don't be surprised if you receive a note from the college president accompanying your child's tuition bill explaining that the tuition increase was necessitated by the new tax law. Whether the increase was actually due to the new law or not, it is an excuse you are bound to hear many times in the future.

Colleges are fearful that the changes in the charitable deduction will mean fewer charitable contributions to the university. In addition, private colleges will have tougher limits on the amount of tax-exempt bonds they can issue, forcing them either to cut back on building plans or to resort to more costly financing through taxable bonds.

Social Security Numbers for Children

A new rite of passage for the nation's youth will be created by the new tax law. When a child turns five years old, he will need a Social Security number.

For some years now, many parents have needed to get their small children Social Security numbers if they opened bank accounts in their names. But the new law will require all children who are at least five years old and claimed as dependents on their parents' tax return to have a "taxpayer identification number" (TIN), which is generally a Social Security number. In back rooms, congressional tax aides referred to this new rule as "TINs for Tots." Parents will have to report the child's TIN or Social Security number on their tax return in order to claim the dependency exemption for him or her. (You will still be able to claim the dependency exemption for children under five years of age without obtaining or reporting a Social Security number for them.)

The reason for the new requirement is that too many parents have been claiming more dependent exemptions on their returns than they are entitled to. By requiring parents to list the Social Security number of each dependent who is at least five years old, the IRS hopes to largely solve the problem and save the Treasury some money. Solving the problem is especially important now that personal exemptions will nearly double, to $2,000, under the new law.

The requirement goes into effect for returns due on or after January 1, 1988.

Failure to include the Social Security number on a return will draw a $5 penalty.

To apply for a Social Security number, you should phone or write your local Social Security office for application form SS-5.

13

INDIVIDUAL RETIREMENT ACCOUNTS (IRAs)

Who Is and Isn't Allowed an IRA Deduction

Just as Individual Retirement Accounts were becoming a staple of the family investment portfolio, Congress decided to scale back the benefits for millions of middle- and upper-income taxpayers who are covered by retirement plans at work.

Every worker still will be able to put money every year into an IRA where it still can grow and compound tax-free until withdrawn. But many people will no longer be able to claim an IRA deduction on their tax returns, beginning with 1987 returns, which are due April 15, 1988.

Whether you are able to claim an IRA deduction or not will depend on your income and whether you are covered by a retirement plan at work.

IF YOU ARE NOT COVERED BY AN EMPLOYER RETIREMENT PLAN

If neither you nor your spouse is covered by some sort of employer retirement plan you will be able to continue to claim a full IRA deduction, regardless of your income. Congress wanted to maintain the full IRA benefits for people who had no other retirement plan to turn to, no matter how well they were paid.

As under the old law, each worker is allowed to contribute up to $2,000 of earnings into an IRA every year and deduct that amount on their tax return. For two-earner couples, each spouse is permitted to contribute up to $2,000, for a combined maximum deposit of $4,000. One-income couples are allowed to make a tax-deductible contribution of up to $2,250.

WHAT IT MEANS TO BE COVERED BY A PENSION PLAN

You are considered covered (the statute actually reads "active participant") by an employer pension plan as soon as you are eligible to participate in the plan. If you are, you are considered covered for IRA purposes even though you may not yet be "vested" in the plan and have nonforfeitable rights to the pension benefits accrued on your behalf.

Employer plans include any qualified pension, profit-sharing, or stock bonus plan; 401(k) plan; qualified annuity plan; Simplified Employee Pension Plan (SEP); tax-sheltered annuity plan; or 501(c)(18) union pension trust.

You are considered an active participant in a profit-sharing or stock bonus plan if any employer contribution is made on your behalf during the year. With regard to a 401(k) plan, you are considered an active participant if you make contributions to the plan, even if the employer does not contribute.

If you are married, and either you or your spouse is covered by an employer plan, then both of you are considered covered for purposes of the IRA provision.

PEOPLE COVERED BY A COMPANY PENSION PLAN

If either you or your spouse is covered by a pension plan at work, you still may be able to claim an IRA deduction depending on your income. If your adjusted gross income (before subtracting the IRA contribution) is below $40,000 on a joint return or less than $25,000 for individuals, then you can take a full IRA deduction just as in the past—regardless of whether you are covered by a pension plan. (For married individuals filing separately, the income threshold is zero. This was done to prevent couples from trying to circumvent the income guidelines by filing separate returns.)

For couples with incomes between $40,000 and $50,000, and individuals with incomes between $25,000 and $35,000, a partial IRA deduction is allowed. The amount of the deduction is reduced proportionately over the $10,000 range. As a rule of thumb, the deduction is reduced $1 for every $5 of income in excess of $40,000 on a joint return and in excess of $25,000 on an individual's return. For example, an individual with income of $30,000 could claim a maximum deduction of $1,000.

But Congress had mercy and set a floor of $200 so that even if you are at the upper end of the income range for partial deductions you will still be able to claim up to a $200 deduction. For example, an individual with income of $34,500 would still be able to deduct up to $200, even though the regular formula would otherwise have limited his deduction to $100.

DEDUCTIONS NOT WORTH AS MUCH AS BEFORE

Even if you are eligible for a full IRA deduction, keep in mind that the tax savings will no longer be as plentiful. The IRA deduction, like all deductions under the new law, is reduced in value by the lower tax rates. Under the old law, a $2,000 IRA deduction saved a person in the 40-percent tax bracket $800 in taxes. Under the new law, this person will be in the 28-percent bracket and save only $560 in taxes.

IRA TABLE 1: How Much a $2,000 IRA Deduction Will Cut Your Tax Bill

IMPACT ON TAX BILLS OF TAXPAYERS ELIGIBLE TO CLAIM AN IRA DEDUCTION

TAX BRACKET	TAX SAVINGS	OUT-OF-POCKET COST OF MAKING CONTRIBUTION
15%	$300	$1,700
28%	$560	$1,440
33%	$660	$1,340
35%*	$700	$1,300
38.5%*	$770	$1,230

* Top rates of 35 percent and 38.5 percent are in effect for 1987 only.

NON-DEDUCTIBLE CONTRIBUTIONS STILL ALLOWED BY ALL WORKERS

Even if you are not allowed to claim any IRA deduction, you are still allowed to put up to $2,000 a year into an IRA ($2,250 for one-income couples, and a combined $4,000 for two-earner couples). You will still gain the benefit of having the money grow and compound tax-free until withdrawn.

If your company offers a 401(k) plan, however, you may be able to do even better. You get the equivalent of an IRA deduction and the money grows tax-free until withdrawn. What's more, you can put even more into a

401(k) and save even more in taxes than you can with an IRA. As a bonus, companies will often match employee contributions to 401(k)s. (See Chapter 14.)

NEW LAW EFFECTIVE IN 1987

The new IRA restrictions are effective beginning in the 1987 tax year. Thus, all workers will still be able to claim an IRA deduction on their 1986 tax returns, due April 15, 1987, as long as the contribution is made by April 15, 1987.

WITHDRAWING MONEY

As was the case under the old law, money in an IRA doesn't get taxed until it's withdrawn, at which time it becomes subject to tax at regular rates. Contributions you made for which you did not get a deduction won't be subject to tax on withdrawal. Only interest, dividends, and other amounts earned on the money will be taxed on withdrawal.

PENALTY FOR EARLY WITHDRAWALS

As under the old law, if you withdraw money before reaching age fifty-nine and a half, become disabled, or die, a 10-percent penalty is imposed. That penalty is in addition to any regular tax owed. The penalty doesn't apply to withdrawals of non-deductible contributions you made to the IRA. But earnings on those contributions are subject to the penalty.

Under the new law, the penalty is waived for withdrawals made before age fifty-nine and a half if taken in equal installments as a lifetime annuity. This new exception applies beginning in 1987.

AMERICAN GOLD AND SILVER COINS NOW ELIGIBLE

Gold and silver coins issued by the United States Government become eligible investments for IRAs under the new law. But other coins, precious metals, stamps, and other collectibles remain off-limits for IRAs, as under the old law.

BORROWING FOR AN IRA DEPOSIT

Congress left alone the provision allowing people to borrow money to make an IRA deposit. In the past, some people who were strapped for cash but who wanted to claim an IRA deduction borrowed the money. Even with the interest payments on the loan, they often came out ahead because of the tax savings resulting from the deduction, the deductibility of the loan interest, and the benefit of having the IRA money grow and compound tax-free.

But many fewer people will find any benefit in borrowing to make IRA contributions in the future, particularly those who are no longer able to claim an IRA deduction. Many of them are likely to come out behind. Even those who are still eligible to claim a deduction may end up losing more than they gain from borrowing because the value of all the tax benefits—the IRA tax deduction, the investment-interest deduction, and the benefit of tax deferral on IRA earnings—is reduced because of the lower tax rates.

New Investment Strategies for IRAs

IRAs have always been an advantageous place to put high-yielding investments, such as bonds or bank certificates of deposit. But tax advisers sometimes used to caution their clients against putting long-term growth stocks into an IRA. That, they said, would be wasteful. Outside an IRA, stocks were taxed at favorable long-term capital-gains rates. But inside an IRA the profits eventually would be taxed more harshly at regular rates when the money was withdrawn.

Under the new law, however, IRAs might be an ideal place for equity investments, says Andrew E. Zuckerman, a tax manager at the accounting firm of Arthur Andersen & Company and a former IRS attorney. Since preferential capital-gains treatment will be eliminated, and stock market profits will be taxed at regular rates, IRAs will provide a refuge where taxes on the profits can be deferred for years. And when the money is withdrawn, it will be taxed no more harshly than if it had remained outside an IRA.

DOES IT STILL MAKE SENSE TO CONTRIBUTE TO IRAs?

If you view the IRA as a long-term retirement account, as Congress intended, it will continue to be an attractive place to put your money. Even without the deduction, IRAs will still be advantageous because the money will grow faster than if left in a regular savings account where the earnings are taxed away each year.

IRA Table 2 compares the after-tax returns of a regular savings account, deductible and non-deductible IRAs, and municipal bonds. The example is based on a taxpayer in the 28-percent tax bracket who makes yearly contributions and doesn't withdraw the money before age fifty-nine and a half, so no early-withdrawal penalty is imposed. Each of the accounts yields 8 percent except for municipal bonds, which yield 6 percent.

As you would expect, being able to claim an IRA deduction is most valuable. A person who earmarked $2,000 of his salary for an IRA would have the full $2,000 working for him, since the deduction would offset any tax normally owed on the salary income.

To make a true comparison, the examples in the table show only $1,440 of the $2,000 salary deposited each year into a regular savings account, non-deductible IRA account, and municipal bond purchases. That is because 28 percent of the $2,000 salary would be subject to tax, leaving only $1,440 to deposit after taxes. Although this may seem confusing, particularly if you plan to put a full $2,000 in, it is the only way to make a valid comparison between the deductible IRA and the other investments.

As long as you don't withdraw money early from the IRA and the 10-percent penalty is avoided, both the deductible IRA and the non-deductible IRA continue to provide a greater return than a regular savings account. Except in the short-term, even non-deductible IRAs fare better than municipal bonds yielding 6 percent.

If the spread between the IRA and the municipal bond was closer, however, the choice between a non-deductible IRA and municipal bonds would be tougher. High state taxes might tilt the scales in favor of municipal bonds. So you'll need to make some calculations.

IRAs No Longer Suitable as a Short-Term Savings Account

In the past some people viewed IRAs as short-term savings accounts, rather than long-term retirement plans. They used IRAs to save for a few years for such things as a boat, a down payment on a second home, or a dream vacation. Even if they had to pay a 10-percent penalty for pulling the money out before reaching age fifty-nine and a half, they found the tax advantages of the IRA produced greater returns than a conventional account after five to eight years or so. But that break-even point will come much later under the new law because the value of the deduction and the tax deferral is diminished. The break-even period is even longer for those who aren't eligible to claim an IRA deduction.

To find out the new break-even points, Mr. Zuckerman of Arthur Andersen conducted an analysis comparing a regular savings account and IRA, both yielding 8 percent (see IRA Table 3). For a taxpayer in the 28-percent tax bracket who claimed an IRA deduction each year, it would take thirteen years before the IRA earned enough to offset the 10-percent penalty and overtook the regular savings account. For a taxpayer who couldn't claim an IRA deduction, the break-even point was nineteen years. These people would have been better off investing the money in municipal bonds for those periods.

Of course, if you are over age fifty-nine and a half, the penalty won't apply, and the IRA will always surpass a regular savings account.

IRA TABLE 2: COMPARING ALTERNATIVE INVESTMENTS

PEOPLE WHO DON'T INCUR AN EARLY IRA WITHDRAWAL PENALTY

[Taxpayers in 28-Percent Tax Bracket; Same Amount Deposited Each Year]

YEAR WITHDRAWN	REGULAR SAVINGS 8% Yield	DEDUCTIBLE IRA 8% Yield	NON-DEDUCTIBLE IRA 8% Yield	MUNICIPAL BOND 6% Yield
Deposit	$ 1,440	$ 2,000	$ 1,440	$ 1,440
5	$ 9,984	$ 10,564	$ 10,025	$ 10,044
10	$ 21,289	$ 23,970	$ 21,693	$ 21,559
15	$ 36,247	$ 43,667	$ 37,891	$ 36,968
20	$ 56,038	$ 72,609	$ 60,746	$ 57,590
30	$116,875	$177,618	$140,384	$122,114

NOTE 1: Amounts for each year represent withdrawals after taxes.
NOTE 2: To make valid comparisons, a full $2,000 contribution is made each year only to the deductible IRA accounts. Deposits to other accounts have to be made with after-tax dollars, so only $1,440 ($2,000 − 28-percent tax) is contributed each year.
SOURCE: Computations by Arthur Andersen & Company

IRA TABLE 3: COMPARING ALTERNATIVE INVESTMENTS (WITH WITHDRAWAL PENALTY)

PEOPLE WHO INCUR A 10-PERCENT EARLY IRA WITHDRAWAL PENALTY

[Taxpayers in 28-Percent Tax Bracket; Same Amount Deposited Each Year]

YEAR WITHDRAWN	REGULAR SAVINGS 8% Yield	DEDUCTIBLE IRA 8% Yield	NON-DEDUCTIBLE IRA 8% Yield	MUNICIPAL BOND 6% Yield
Deposit	$ 1,440	$ 2,000	$ 1,440	$ 1,440
5	$ 9,984	$ 9,097	$ 9,833	$ 10,044
10	$ 21,289	$ 20,640	$ 20,880	$ 21,559
13	$ 29,757	$ 30,027	$ 29,280	$ 30,262
14	$ 32,911	$ 33,669	$ 32,449	$ 33,517
15	$ 36,247	$ 37,602	$ 35,829	$ 36,968
18	$ 47,452	$ 51,393	$ 47,400	$ 48,614
19	$ 51,625	$ 56,745	$ 51,800	$ 52,971
20	$ 56,038	$ 62,524	$ 56,509	$ 57,590
30	$116,875	$152,949	$127,086	$122,114

NOTE 1: Amounts for each year represent withdrawals after taxes. IRA amounts include impact of 10-percent premature withdrawal penalty.

NOTE 2: To make valid comparisons, a full $2,000 contribution is made each year only to the deductible IRA accounts. Deposits to other accounts have to be made with after-tax dollars, so only $1,440 ($2,000 − 28-percent tax) is contributed each year.

SOURCE: Computations by Arthur Andersen & Company

14

401(k) EMPLOYEE RETIREMENT PLANS AND KEOGH PLANS

401(k)s

Salary Reduction Plans, more commonly known as 401(k) plans for the governing section of the Internal Revenue Code, have in a few short years become one of most popular employee retirement savings plans. And despite some new limitations, these plans are likely to become even more popular because of the new restrictions on Individual Retirement Accounts.

Since Congress created 401(k)s in 1978, a fast-growing number of companies have established these plans as a way of encouraging employees to save for their own retirement. The plans, which are sometimes referred to as "cash-or-deferred arrangements," have been popular among employees because they offer the same generous tax benefits as IRAs—and often much more.

Contributing to a 401(k) plan will reduce your current income tax bill, and the money is allowed to earn interest and grow tax-free as long as it remains in the plan. Only when the money is withdrawn does it become subject to tax.

Under a 401(k) employees are allowed to earmark a portion of their salary for deposit to the plan each year. No income tax has to be paid on the amount contributed. So if you earn $40,000 a year and you decide to contribute $2,000 of it to a 401(k), only $38,000 of your salary is subject to income tax.

That is the same as receiving a $2,000 deduction for an IRA contribution. The only difference is that with a 401(k), the $2,000 contribution will not even show up as income on your W-2 form, so you don't even report it as part of your gross income on your tax return. (The money, however, is subject to Social Security taxes.) With an IRA, you would report receiving gross income of $40,000 on your tax return, and then, if eligible, claim a deduction of $2,000. Either way, only $38,000 of your salary would be subject to taxes.

Thus, people who are no longer eligible to claim a deduction for an IRA will be able to turn to 401(k)s for the same type of tax relief. The benefits are the same. That is why many companies without 401(k) plans will undoubtedly feel pressure from employees who are not eligible to claim an IRA deduction to establish a 401(k) plan.

What makes 401(k)s even better than IRAs is that people can contribute even more than $2,000 to a 401(k), providing them an opportunity to reduce their tax bill even further. What's more, many companies will match employee contributions to the plan.

The maximum amount an employee can earmark to a 401(k) plan beginning in 1987 is $7,000 a year. That compares with a limit of $30,000 a year under the old law. Even though the limit has been sharply reduced, only a small percentage of employees—usually well-paid executives—ever put in more than $7,000 a year into a 401(k). Beginning in 1988 the $7,000 ceiling will be increased to take account of inflation.

Not all employees are permitted to contribute the maximum $7,000. As under the old law, employees are allowed to put in no more than 20 percent of their compensation, up to the $7,000 maximum. Thus, someone with compensation of $35,000 or more can contribute the maximum $7,000 ($35,000 x 20 percent = $7,000). But a worker earning, say, $25,000 would be limited to a contribution of $5,000 a year ($25,000 x 20 percent = $5,000).

(Incidentally, the statute actually stipulates 25 percent of compensation, rather than 20 percent. But compensation is defined as compensation after the 401(k) contribution has been subtracted from gross pay. That requires a bit of algebra to figure your maximum allowable contribution. For those who do not remember their high-school algebra, a rule of thumb is to use 20 percent of gross pay.)

Keep in mind that these are the limits imposed by the tax law. For various reasons, employers often impose even lower limits on the amount employees can contribute, such as 5 percent to 15 percent of their salary.

The new law also places special restrictions on the amount that can be contributed by higher-paid employees based on amounts contributed by other employees in the plan.

Money placed in a 401(k) plan is usually invested by outside financial institutions hired by your company to administer the plan.

Although 401(k) plans may proliferate in the private sector, they will come to a screeching halt in the public sector. The new law allows 401(k) plans set up by state and local governments before May 6, 1986, to continue. Employees covered under these previously established plans would be able to continue to put money away in these plans every year and enjoy all the benefits.

But no new 401(k) plans can be set up by a state or local government for their employees after that date.

Tax-exempt organizations also don't have a chance to set up new 401(k)s for their employees. Only plans that were adopted before July 1, 1986, are protected, or "grandfathered," and allowed to continue for the benefit of their employees.

NEW WITHDRAWAL RESTRICTIONS

Withdrawals from a 401(k) plan are generally permitted only when you retire, die, become disabled, leave the company, reach age fifty-nine and a half, or suffer a financial hardship. The IRS has not spelled out exactly what financial hardships are covered. Thus, employers have been left the task of deciding whether a withdrawal should be allowed for an employee who is pressed for funds to buy a new house or pay a child's college tuition.

The new law still allows early withdrawals for hardships, but beginning in 1987 you will generally incur a 10-percent penalty on top of the regular tax due on withdrawals. Hardship withdrawals made to pay deductible medical expenses are exempt from the penalty. Under the old law, the penalty applied only to individuals who were 5 percent, or more, owners of the business.

In addition, the new law limits the amount you can withdraw for hardships to your personal contributions to the plan. Beginning in 1989, you won't be able to withdraw earnings from the plan as you could under the old law.

The difficulty of withdrawing funds early from a 401(k) makes these plans less flexible than IRAs. Although you may be stuck paying an early withdrawal penalty, you can always gain access to your IRA funds.

Keogh Plans

Self-employed individuals will find Keogh retirement plans virtually unchanged by the new tax law. The one major change is that people who contribute to Keogh plans will no longer be able to claim an additional deduction for IRA contributions unless your income is below the prescribed levels—$50,000 on a joint return and $35,000 for individuals.

Keogh plans are like IRAs in that deposits are tax-deductible and money in the plan is allowed to grow and compound tax-free until withdrawn. The big difference is that Keogh plans also offer you an opportunity to deduct much more than an IRA. Anyone with self-employment income qualifies to set up a Keogh plan, including people with sideline businesses.

The limits on deductible contributions were left unchanged by the new law. If you set up what is known as a "money-purchase" Keogh plan, you can make a tax-deductible deposit each year of up to 20 percent of your net self-employment earnings, up to a maximum of $30,000. This type of plan requires you to contribute a fixed percentage of your income each year.

If you have a "profit-sharing" Keogh plan, which allows you to vary the size of your contributions from year to year, the tax-deductible limit is 13.043 percent of your self-employment earnings, up to a maximum deposit of $30,000.

With Keogh plans, you have until the due date of your tax return—including filing extensions—to make a contribution to the plan and claim a tax deduction on your return. In other words, you can make a deposit even later than April 15 provided you have an extension to file your return. But the plan must have been set up by December 31 for the tax year in question. For example, for a deposit to qualify for a tax deduction on your 1986 tax return, due April 15, 1987, the plan must be set up by December 31, 1986. But you would have until April 15, 1987—or until the extended due date of your return—to make the deposit and claim the deduction on your 1986 return.

15

INVESTMENTS

Investments: An Overview

The investment landscape gets markedly changed by the new tax law, diminishing the returns of some investments while enhancing the yields of others.

Investments that had no special tax advantages under the old law, such as bank accounts, money market funds, and corporate bonds, benefit from the reduction in individual tax rates. By contrast, tax shelters, real estate, and other investments will lose many of the tax benefits that have long enticed investors. Stocks, gold, antiques, and other collectibles will no longer benefit from long-term capital-gains tax treatment.

Nevertheless, the new tax law will not necessarily radically reorder the relative attractiveness of the full spectrum of investments. After all, tax benefits represent only a part of the return of most investments. Stock market investors, for example, are not likely to sell all their holdings and put all their money in the bank just because bank accounts will be taxed more lightly than before and stocks will lose their favorable capital-gains treatment. Nobody ever got rich from putting their money in a bank account. Thus, investors are likely to continue to look to the stock market and elsewhere for the big profits, even though the profits may not be quite as large in the future because of the harsher tax treatment.

To be sure, some investments whose tax advantages have been a major part of their return, such as in the case of tax shelters, will lose much of their appeal. But some adjustments might occur that would at least partially make up for the loss of tax benefits. For example, many investors might initially shun real estate because of the cutback in tax benefits. But that might lead to a slowdown in new construction and eventually force rents higher as housing supplies tightened. Should that happen, the higher rents would help offset the loss of the tax benefits.

The tax changes, in making some investments more attractive and others less attractive, will have a marked impact on asset values and yields. Some adjustments have already occurred. Property values of investment real estate in many parts of the country have already declined because of the cutback in tax benefits. And the stocks of companies that stand to see their fortunes increased by the new law have been bid up in price, while those that would be hurt have been pulled down in price.

Capital Gains—The End of Preferential Treatment

For owners of stock, real estate, gold, collectibles, and a variety of other such investments, the tax code has long provided preferential tax treatment for patient investors who hold onto their assets awhile before selling them. The tax reform law completely abolishes the favored treatment.

All profits from the sale of stock, real estate, and other capital assets will be taxed just like wages. It does not matter whether you hold the asset two days, six months, or ten years. All profits get taxed the same. Patient investors will no longer get a special break on the rates.

Many investors will no doubt be disappointed by the change because for many decades the tax code provided quite a tax break. Under the old law, if you held an asset for more than six months before selling it, you were allowed to exempt 60 percent of the profit from tax and you had to pay tax on only 40 percent of the gain. For someone in the top 50-percent bracket, that made for a top effective rate on these "long-term capital gains" of 20 percent (50 percent x 40 percent of gain = 20-percent effective rate). Under the new law, this person would be paying tax on the gain at a rate of 28 percent or as much as 33 percent after 1987.

Many people who were paying even lower capital-gains rates under the old law will also see their effective rate jump to 28 percent. For example, a single person who was in the 30-percent tax bracket under the old law and paid an effective long-term capital-gain rate of 12 percent (30-percent bracket x 40 percent of gain = 12 percent effective rate) will see their capital-gain rate more than double, to 28 percent, under the new law.

A married couple in the 25-percent tax bracket under the old law who paid an effective rate of 10 percent on long-term gains would see their capital-gains rate rise to 15 percent under the new law.

SHORT-TERM GAINS BENEFIT FROM NEW LAW

There is a silver lining: Short-term capital gains will be taxed much less harshly. Under the old law, if you held a stock or other asset for six months or less, you had to pay tax on the profit at regular rates of up to 50 percent. There was no special break. Profits were taxed just like other income.

Under the new law, all gains are taxed just like other income, but the rates are much lower—at 15 percent, 28 percent, or 33 percent. Thus, people who were paying rates of, say, 40 percent or 50 percent on their short-term profits will be taxed at rates of no more than 28 percent or 33 percent under the new law. Many people who were paying rates of 20 percent or 30 percent on their short-term profits will be paying only a 15-percent rate under the new law.

The bottom line is that all capital gains will be treated the same under the new law. There is no distinction between short-term and long-term gains. No matter how long you own the asset before selling it, your profits are taxed just like your wages and other types of taxable income.

MAKING THE TRANSITION IN 1987

The old law rules on capital gains fully apply for 1986. In 1987 there is a transition between the old and new rules.

In 1987, as previously mentioned, there are five rate brackets of 11 percent, 15 percent, 28 percent, 35 percent, and 38.5 percent. For people who are in the 11-percent, 15-percent, or 28-percent tax brackets, the new law takes full effect. Any capital gains they have—be they short-term or long-term—will be taxed just like their other income at rates of 11 percent, 15 percent, or 28 percent.

But for people in the 35-percent or 38.5-percent brackets, the distinction between long-term and short-term gains will still be important for 1987. The reason is that Congress wanted to prevent long-term capital gains from being taxed at a rate higher than 28 percent during the transition. Lawmakers feared a chilling impact on investment might result if the effective rate on long-term gains were allowed to jump from 20 percent in 1986 to a top rate of 38.5 percent in 1987. So they decided to cap long-term gains at 28 percent for 1987.

Thus, if you are in the 35-percent or 38.5-percent brackets, your long-term gains will be taxed at rates no higher than 28 percent. But that cap applies only to long-term gains. If you sell a stock that was held six months or less, the cap would not apply. So your profits would be taxed at 35 percent or 38.5 percent. As a result you will need to keep the distinction between long-term and short-term gains in mind until the end of 1987. If you forget, it could mean the difference between paying 28 percent and 35 percent or 38.5 percent.

In 1988 the distinction disappears. But upper-income people in the top bracket could see their top rate on capital gains rise from 28 percent to 33 percent. As discussed earlier, while the top rate in the new tax system is advertised as being 28 percent, there is a hidden 33-percent rate that upper-income taxpayers have to pay on part of their income above a certain threshold beginning in 1988.

CAPITAL-GAINS TAX RATES

1986

REGULAR TAX BRACKET	EFFECTIVE CAPITAL GAIN RATE	
	Short-term Gain	*Long-term Gain*
11%	11%	4.4%
12%	12%	4.8%
14%	14%	5.6%
15%	15%	6.0%
16%	16%	6.4%
17%	17%	6.8%
18%	18%	7.2%
20%	20%	8.0%
22%	22%	8.8%
23%	23%	9.2%
24%	24%	9.6%
25%	25%	10.0%
26%	26%	10.4%
28%	28%	11.2%
30%	30%	12.0%
32%	32%	12.8%
33%	33%	13.2%
34%	34%	13.6%
35%	35%	14.0%
38%	38%	15.2%
42%	42%	16.8%
45%	45%	18.0%
48%	48%	19.2%
49%	49%	19.6%
50%	50%	20.0%

CAPITAL-GAINS TAX RATES

1987

REGULAR TAX BRACKET	EFFECTIVE CAPITAL GAIN RATE	
	Short-term Gain	*Long-term Gain*
11%	11%	11%
15%	15%	15%
28%	28%	28%
35%	35%	28%
38.5%	38.5%	28%

1988

REGULAR TAX BRACKET	EFFECTIVE CAPITAL GAIN RATE
	Short- or Long-term
15%	15%
28%	28%
33%*	33%
28%	28%

* Some upper-income taxpayers face a 33-percent marginal tax rate on part of their income above a certain level, reflecting the phase-out of the benefit of the 15-percent tax bracket and personal exemptions. (The 33-percent rate kicks in at taxable income of $71,900 on joint returns, $43,150 on single returns, $61,650 for heads of household, and $35,950 for married persons filing separately.) Thus, part of their capital gains might be subject to tax at this 33-percent rate. When the phase-outs are completed (e.g., at taxable income of $192,930 in 1988 for a married couple with two children, or $100,480 for a single person), the marginal rate drops back to 28-percent on income in excess of those levels, and thus capital gains above those levels would be taxed at an effective rate of 28 percent.

MAKES INVESTMENT DECISIONS SIMPLER

Although you will pay higher taxes on your long-term gains under the new law, taxing all gains alike will make investment decisions much simpler. You won't have to worry about how long you have held the asset when deciding when to sell. Under the old law, many investors were most reluctant to sell a stock before the six-month holding period ended because they didn't want to pay the higher taxes on a short-term gain. Many held on dearly until the six months was up, even if they were concerned that the stock might head downward. And for some of them, that is exactly what happened. Their stock fell more in price than they gained from waiting the six months for the favorable tax treatment.

Since long-term gains will no longer receive favorable tax treatment, you can sell a stock whenever you think the time is ripe. If you want to run with your profits after holding on to it only two hours, two days, two weeks, or five years, the tax treatment is the same. The new law will allow the decision as to when to sell to be guided merely by the investment merits, not the tax consequences.

WHAT CONGRESS AND WALL STREET WERE THINKING

Congress felt that with individual tax rates being reduced to such low levels, the need to provide a special reduced rate for capital gains as an investment incentive was eliminated. Many liberal Democrats have long questioned why profits from certain investments should be treated more favorably by the tax code than wages from the sweat of labor.

Wall Street protested the elimination of the preferential treatment, but there was no loud outcry. Many brokers foresaw the potential for increased trading activity—and thus increased commissions for themselves—if the distinction between long-term and short-term gains was eliminated and the top rate on short-term gains was significantly reduced. They figured that investors might buy and sell more frequently with the rate on short-term gains reduced and the incentive gone to hold onto their stocks for more than six months. Indeed, your broker might try putting the pressure on you now to sell early more often. While you no longer have the excuse of waiting six months for the long-term capital-gains rates, don't let the broker try to churn your account.

ONE TAX BENEFIT REMAINS

There is still one tax advantage that investors who own stocks or other capital assets will continue to enjoy: the benefit of being able to defer taxes on gains until the asset is sold. While many people take this treatment for granted, it is, indeed, an advantage. Income from other investments, such as interest, dividends, and royalties, are taxed every year. Certainly, one reason why the federal government doesn't tax increases in the value of stock, gold, and other capital assets every year is that those gains may never be realized; the price of the stock could fall. But for assets that do continue to appreciate in value, the tax deferral is a real benefit.

CAPITAL GAINS—STATE TAX IMPACT

The impact of the repeal of capital gains treatment will be even more pronounced when state and local income taxes are taken into account for people living in states that follow the federal system and will no longer offer preferential capital gains treatment either. The table below shows the combined effect of federal and state taxes in states that impose taxes on capital gains. The federal rate used in the calculations is 28 percent.

THE COMBINED IMPACT OF FEDERAL AND STATE TAXES ON CAPITAL GAINS

MAXIMUM EFFECTIVE INDIVIDUAL CAPITAL GAINS TAX RATES
[Adjusted for Effect of Federal Deductibility]

STATE	HIGHEST STATE BRACKET (%)	EFFECTIVE OLD TAX (%)	EFFECTIVE NEW TAX (%)
New York	13.5	22.7	37.72
Iowa	13.0	22.6	37.36
West Virginia	13.0	22.6	37.36
California	11.0	22.2	35.92
DC	11.0	22.2	35.92
Hawaii	11.0	22.2	35.92
Montana	11.0	22.2	35.92
Delaware	9.8	21.96	35.26
Maine	10.0	22.0	35.2
Massachusetts	10.0	22.0	35.2
Oregon	10.0	22.0	35.2
Minnesota	14.0	22.8	35.08
Kansas	9.0	21.8	34.48
North Dakota	9.0	21.8	34.48
New Mexico	8.5	21.56	34.12
Ohio	8.3	21.66	34.0
Arizona	8.0	21.6	33.76
Colorado	8.0	21.6	33.76
Wisconsin	7.9	21.58	33.69
Maryland	5.0	21.5	33.6
Utah	7.75	21.56	33.58
Idaho	7.5	21.56	33.4
Arkansas	7.0	21.4	33.04
Connecticut	7.0	23.5	33.04
South Carolina	7.0	21.4	33.04
Georgia	6.0	21.2	32.32
Kentucky	6.0	21.1	32.32
Louisiana	6.0	21.2	32.32
Missouri	6.0	21.2	32.32

THE COMBINED IMPACT OF FEDERAL AND STATE TAXES ON CAPITAL GAINS

MAXIMUM EFFECTIVE INDIVIDUAL CAPITAL GAINS TAX RATES
[Adjusted for Effect of Federal Deductibility]

STATE	HIGHEST STATE BRACKET (%)	EFFECTIVE OLD TAX (%)	EFFECTIVE NEW TAX (%)
Oklahoma	6.0	21.2	32.32
Virginia	5.75	21.13	32.14
Nebraska	5.4	21.08	31.9
Michigan	4.6	21.0	31.32
New Jersey	3.5	20.7	30.52
Indiana	3.0	20.6	30.16
Illinois	2.5	21.25	29.8
Rhode Island	22.21% of federal		
Vermont	26.50% of federal		

STATES THAT HAVE NO CAPITAL-GAINS TAX

Alabama	Mississippi	North Carolina	Tennessee
Alaska	Nevada	Pennsylvania	Texas
Florida	New Hampshire	South Dakota	Washington
			Wyoming

NOTE: Table assumes that all states will repeal existing preferences for capital gains. The top federal rate used in the computations is 28 percent for 1987.

SOURCE: Cesar V. Conda, tax economist at the U.S. Chamber of Commerce.

WIDE VARIETY OF ASSETS COVERED

The changes affect a wide variety of investments, including profits from the sale of stock, bonds, options, incentive stock options granted to executives, real estate, gold, silver, antiques, gems, timber, rare coins, stamps, and other collectibles.

CAPITAL LOSSES

Although preferential tax treatment is abolished for capital gains, the new law still limits the amount of losses you can claim each year. The new limits are the same that applied under the old law. You can use losses to offset any gains you have, plus up to $3,000 to offset other income. For example, say you had a bad year in the stock market and you had only $5,000 in capital gains and $20,000 in losses. You would be able to claim only $8,000 in losses ($5,000 to offset the $5,000 in gains plus $3,000 to offset other income). The $12,000 in losses that you couldn't use could be carried forward and used in a future year—subject to the same limitations that no more than $3,000 in net losses can be deducted from other income in any year.

Of course, many people thought it was unfair for Congress to get rid of preferential treatment for long-term capital gains while keeping the old law's limits on losses. But revenue considerations dictated that the limit on losses be retained.

There was one change made to the treatment of losses. The distinction between long-term and short-term losses disappears. Under the old law, losses from long-term investments were only half as valuable as short-term losses. While net short-term losses could be used to offset other income dollar-for-dollar, up to the $3,000 limit, it took $2 of net long-term losses to offset $1 of other income. Thus, you needed to $6,000 in long-term losses to offset $3,000 in other income.

Since the distinction between long-term and short-term losses disappears under the new law, net losses from either long-term or short-term investments can be used dollar-for-dollar to offset other income, up to $3,000.

Stocks

The new tax law holds good news and bad news for stocks. High-yielding stocks paying high dividends become more attractive under the new law because of the reduction in individual tax rates. Dividends are taxed at much lower rates. By contrast, high-growth stocks will be hurt by the repeal of long-term capital-gains tax treatment.

But the news is not all good for high-yielding stocks nor all bad for growth stocks. Smaller investors may find the benefit of the lower tax rate offset by the loss of the special dividend exclusion. Beginning in 1987 the tax exclusion for the first $100 in dividends ($200 on a joint return) is eliminated.

Meanwhile, people who like to move swiftly in and out of the market and sell their growth stocks after a quick run-up in price will fare much better under the new law because short-term capital gains will get taxed at lower rates. Short-term gains get taxed just like long-term gains.

Patient investors who tend to look toward the long term in growth stocks may feel like they got the short end of the stick with the repeal of long-term capital-gains treatment. Nevertheless, growth stocks will maintain their appeal because appreciation in the price of stocks is usually where the big money is made.

Despite the loss of capital-gains tax treatment, the stock market may attract even more money than in the past because many investors will be looking for places to put some of their money now that tax shelters are much less attractive.

Stock market investors will find the changes in the corporate tax area will significantly alter the after-tax returns of a large cross-section of corporate America. Though the impact will vary from company to company, many high-tech companies, retailers, and service-oriented firms will see their after-tax earnings rise because of the reduction in the corporate tax rate. But taxes may go up for heavy industry, military contractors, large banks, real estate, and some utilities. While stock prices may have adjusted already in anticipation of the changes, keep in mind their future fortunes may be affected by the tax changes.

INSTALLMENT SALES OF STOCKS

Stock market investors will no longer have the option of choosing whether to report their profits from year-end stock sales in the year the sale took place or the following year.

Normally, income has to be reported for the year when it is earned. But the old law provided a limited exception: Investors who sold stocks in the last five trading days of the year had the option of reporting profits on either the return for that taxable year or electing the "installment" method and reporting the gain the following tax year.

The new law will require profits to be recognized in the year the stock was sold. Losses always had to be reported in the same year as the stock was sold. The provision applies to stock sold after 1986.

The new law also eliminates the use of the installment method of reporting for sales of publicly traded stocks, bonds, and other securities beginning in 1987. Some relatively wealthy investors have often used this method in the past.

Bank Accounts

The reduction in individual tax rates will add some luster to the conventional forms of savings accounts at banks, savings and loans, credit unions, and other financial institutions. The after-tax return of the variety of interest-bearing accounts will improve, including the passbook account, certificates of deposit, money market deposit accounts, Christmas club accounts, commercial paper, and the NOW and Super NOW interest-bearing checking accounts.

All these investments will be helped, since their interest is subject to regular tax rates, which will be sharply reduced under the new law. So a customer who was in the 30-percent tax bracket under the old law will likely pay no more than $15 in taxes for every $100 of interest earned under the new law, instead of $30. Someone in the 40-percent bracket under the old law would likely pay no more than $28 in taxes per $100 of interest earned under the new system, a sharp drop from the $40 tax he paid under the old law.

Art, Antiques, Stamps, and Other Collectibles

Investments in objets d'art and other collectibles will be taxed more harshly under the new law because of the loss of favorable long-term capital-gains tax treatment.

The change will affect the whole gamut of collectibles, including fine art, antiques, rare coins, stamps, Oriental rugs, rare books, Chinese ceramics, gold and silver objects, and collections of baseball cards, comic books, and other such items.

The return from these types of investments is exclusively from the increase in the object's value. So their after-tax return will be diminished under the new law because profits on the sale of these assets will be taxed at regular rates of 15 percent, 28 percent, or 33 percent (remember the hidden rate), rather than the lower capital-gains rates.

Only people who tend to turn around and sell collectibles soon after acquiring them will benefit from the new law, since short-term gains will be taxed at lower rates than in the past. But most collectibles are not sold quickly after being acquired. In most cases, collectibles ended up qualifying for favorable long-term capital-gains treatment under the old law, since investors typically hold collectibles for years while waiting for their value to appreciate.

Say, for example, you brought an antique desk ten years ago for $1,000 and you were able to sell it for $10,000. Under the old law, the $9,000 gain would be taxed at a rate no higher than 20 percent, making for a maximum tax of $1,800 on the $9,000 profit. Under the new law, the gain would be taxed at rates as high as 33 percent in 1988, making the tax on the $9,000 profit as high as $2,970. That is a 65-percent increase in tax. The bottom line: You would end up with a profit after taxes of $6,030, compared with $7,200 under the old law.

But this example illustrates well the point that taxes are only one factor in an investment. Even though the tax treatment is harsher, a $6,030 net profit is still a spectacular gain on a $1,000 investment. Someone who is expert in the field and sees great promise for a collectible object is not likely to be deterred by the harsher tax treatment when the rewards can still be large.

Corporate Bonds

Corporate bonds come up winners under the new law. Their after-tax return will be enhanced because interest income will be taxed at lower rates. Gains on the sale of bonds, however, will no longer qualify for favorable long-term capital-gains tax treatment.

Federal Government Bonds

After-tax yields on Treasury bills, bonds, notes, and other federal securities go up under the new law, since interest income will be taxed at lower rates. In addition, interest on Treasury issues, as well as many other federal agency securities, remain exempt from state and local taxes.

Municipal Bonds

With a few exceptions, municipal bonds retain their tax-exempt status, but their advantage over taxable bonds narrows because of the lower individual tax rates. In other words, the tax exemption is not worth as much if the tax bite is smaller.

Yet many people will still find them attractive. How attractive will depend on your tax bracket and the gap between yields on taxable bonds and tax-exempt bonds. Even before the legislation was passed by Congress, municipal bond yields adjusted to levels that made them quite appealing to many people.

Exactly how the market will develop in the future is uncertain. Many forces will come into play. There will be somewhat fewer tax-exempt issues coming to market because of new restrictions placed on the type and amount that can be issued. So the supply of bonds will shrink. But so might demand. Financial institutions, which are major purchasers of municipal bonds, will no longer get an interest deduction for money borrowed to finance their purchase of tax-exempt bonds. Thus, financial institutions are likely to reduce their purchases. But many brokerage houses are trying to stimulate interest among individuals. Brokers are touting municipal bonds as one of the few tax shelters left under the new law.

Whether they are attractive will depend on each individual. You'll have to make some calculations to compare the after-tax returns on both municipal bonds and tax-exempt bonds. The table below provides comparisons of taxable and tax-exempt yields. For example, if you are in the 28-percent tax bracket, a tax-exempt bond yielding 7-percent interest would give you the same return as a taxable bond yielding 9.7 percent. That means that if taxable bonds are paying less than 9.7 percent, the municipal bond is the better deal, other things being equal.

If you are in the 15-percent tax bracket, a 7-percent municipal bond will give you the same return as a taxable bond paying 8.2 percent. So if you find taxable bonds are yielding more than 8.2 percent, the taxable bonds will be the better deal. If your state has an income tax, you should always factor in the benefit of the exemption for state and local taxes, which may increase the advantage of tax-exempt bonds over taxable bonds. Interest is generally exempt from state and local taxes in the state where the bonds are issued. But virtually all states impose taxes on out-of-state bonds held by residents.

COMPARING MUNICIPAL BONDS WITH TAXABLE BONDS

	A TAX-FREE MUNICIPAL BOND THAT YIELDS					
	5%	6%	7%	8%	9%	10%
TAX BRACKET	IS EQUIVALENT TO A TAXABLE BOND YIELD OF					
15%	5.9%	7.1%	8.2%	9.4%	10.6%	11.8%
28%	6.9%	8.3%	9.7%	11.1%	12.5%	13.9%
33%	7.5%	9.0%	10.4%	11.9%	13.4%	14.9%

Under the new law, you are going to have to take a closer look at what you are buying because not all municipal bonds will be completely tax-exempt. Municipal bonds issued by state and local governments for "public purposes," such as schools and roads, generally maintain their tax-exempt status.

But certain municipal bonds issued for private purposes, such as for industrial development, will become subject to the alternative minimum tax. Meanwhile, some other private-purpose bonds will no longer carry a federal tax exemption.

ALTERNATIVE MINIMUM TAX

Some upper-income individuals will find that interest from certain private-purpose tax-exempt bonds issued after August 7, 1986, are subject to the alternative minimum tax. The bonds affected are primarily industrial-development bonds, student-loan bonds, and housing bonds.

If you are investing in a mutual fund, check the bonds in the fund to see if any of them would have to be included in the alternative minimum tax. In the mutual fund industry there has been talk about setting up funds that would stay away from these types of bonds to accommodate those who might be subject to the alternative minimum tax.

Taxpayers who are not vulnerable to the minimum tax may find some benefit in investing in these bonds since they will probably carry a higher yield than other tax-exempt bonds.

TAXABLE MUNICIPAL BONDS

Congress felt that too many tax-exempt bonds were being issued for private purposes, so lawmakers decided to restrict the amount and type of bonds that can be issued. For instance, tax-exempt bonds can no longer be used to finance sports stadiums or convention facilities owned by private interests. And states will face new restrictions on the amount of tax-exempt bonds they can issue for certain purposes, such as multifamily housing construction. They might still issue bonds for these purposes and carry an exemption from state and local income taxes. But some of these issues may not be exempt from federal tax.

To make things even more complicated, the law contains many special exceptions for particular projects. For example, a number of planned sports stadiums across the country were protected from the change in the law and will be allowed to issue tax-exempt bonds.

The bottom line in all this is that you will now have to check carefully to see if the municipal bond you are buying is really exempt from federal taxes.

U.S. Savings Bonds

U.S. Savings Bonds retain their special tax advantages under the new law and may have wider appeal because of their special features.

Federal taxes on the interest can be deferred until you cash in the bond. And the interest is exempt from state and local taxes.

Series EE bonds, the only class of U.S. Savings Bonds that can be purchased with cash today, do not pay interest every six months like most other bonds. Rather, you buy the bond at a discount from its redemption value. The difference is your interest, which you don't get until the bond is redeemed. New bonds mature and reach full redemption value in twelve years.

Savings Bonds have grown in popularity in recent years because their interest rate is adjusted every six months to reflect prevailing interest-rate levels. The yield is set at 85 percent of the average market yield of five-year Treasury notes. Savers are guaranteed a minimum rate of 6.0 percent if the bond is held at least five years. If you cash in the bond before five years, a lower fixed rate applies.

You have the choice of postponing paying federal tax on the interest until you cash in the bond, or paying taxes each year on the interest as it accrues.

Many tax advisers are suggesting that parents consider U.S. Savings Bonds for their younger children because of the change in tax treatment of children under fourteen. Their investment income in excess of $1,000 a year will be taxed at the parents' tax rate. Once the child reaches age fourteen, all the child's income is taxed at his or her own low rate.

As a result, savings bonds can be given to a young child and taxes on the interest can be deferred until the bond matures. By then, the child will be over fourteen and the interest would be taxed at his or her own rate rather than at the parents' higher rate. For young children with investment income under $1,000 a year, parents might consider paying the tax on the bonds annually instead of deferring it, since it would be taxed at the child's low rate. That way you could avoid paying a large amount of deferred taxes when the bond is redeemed.

Keep in mind that the benefit of the tax-deferral feature of Series EE bonds will not be as valuable under the new law because of the lower tax rates. Before investing, you should compare their after-tax return with other types of bonds, including municipal bonds, which are exempt from federal taxes, as well as state and local taxes.

Commodity Futures

Commodity-futures profits get taxed at regular rates, rather than the mixed treatment they got under the old law.

The old law formula treated 60 percent of the profit as a long-term gain and 40 percent as short-term. That made for a maximum tax rate of 32 percent.

The 60-40 regime is retained in the new law, but with the distinction between long-term and short-term gains disappearing, profits will be taxed at regular individual rates of 15 percent, 28 percent, and 33 percent in 1988. In 1987, when the distinction between long-term and short-term capital gains remains for upper-income taxpayers, profits would be taxed at a top effective rate of 32.2 percent.

As under the old law, commodity profits will continue to become taxable at the end of each year even if you have not yet liquidated your position.

Stock Options

Stock options generally gain more favorable tax treatment under the new law. Profits on three- and six-month options, which were always short-term gains and subject to regular tax rates, benefit from the reduction in individual tax rates.

However, nine-month options do not fare as well. Under the old law, they qualified for preferential long-term capital-gains tax treatment if held more than six months. Under the new law, profits will be taxed at regular rates.

Venture Capital

Venture capitalists, investors who invest money in budding new enterprises, will be hurt by the loss of favorable capital-gains tax treatment. Because of the long-term nature of venture-capital investments, profits usually come only in the form of a large long-term capital gain, which will be more harshly taxed under the new law. And losses, which are frequent in this high-risk area of investing, still will be limited in the amount that can be deducted by the capital-loss rules.

In the speculative world of venture capital, investors tend to invest in several new enterprises, hoping that one or two will become big winners over the course of seven to ten years and profits from them will more than offset the losses from the failures. Venture capitalists argued that the preferential tax treatment of capital gains under the old law helped keep the after-tax reward attractive enough to make the risk and the long wait worthwhile.

But the tax changes are not likely to be devastating for venture capital. First, capital-gains rates were at 28 percent as recently as 1981. Second, tax-exempt investors, such as pension funds and foundations, and foreign investors have become a growing force in venture capital in recent years, and these funding sources are unlikely to be affected by any changes in the tax treatment of capital gains.

Further, many people will still be drawn to venture-capital investments by the potential for the big returns that can be had by getting in on the ground floor of a fledgling business.

Cash-Value Life Insurance Policies

Cash-value life insurance policies, such as whole life and universal life, retain their tax advantages under the new law. Investors will be able to continue to defer paying taxes on the annual buildup in the cash surrender value of these policies. Of course, the advantage of this tax deferral will not be as valuable as before because of the lower individual tax rates.

16

TAX SHELTERS

Tax Shelters: An Overview

Under the new tax system, tax shelters—at least in their traditional form —can be expected to pass into extinction. With limited exceptions, doctors, movie stars, professional athletes, and other prosperous individuals will no longer be able to use tax shelters to shield their salary, interest, and dividend income from the tax collector.

Wealthy investors still would be able to find shelter in certain oil- and gas-drilling ventures, but only if they were willing to assume a new element of risk. Investments in low-income housing and historic rehabilitation projects will also offer limited shelter to all but the wealthiest investors. And people with adjusted gross income of up to $150,000 would be allowed to use some tax-shelter losses to offset taxes owed on their other income, but only if they were willing to become landlords of a rental property.

Large syndicates will likely still offer partnership interests in real estate, motion pictures, and equipment-leasing ventures that are typically structured with the smaller investor in mind. But most of these deals are not in the standard mold of a tax shelter because they focus more on generating income than tax deductions. As a result, they tend to produce relatively few, if any, tax losses.

In any case, these deals will be somewhat less attractive under the new law, since any tax losses they do generate would no longer help investors reduce the taxes they owe on other income. Furthermore, the deductions generated, which help reduce the amount of taxes owed on the investment itself, will be scaled back by the new law.

For these reasons, the new law deals a crippling blow to the traditional high-powered shelters that yield huge write-offs for wealthy investors looking to sharply reduce their tax bills. The kinds of shelters that attracted wealthy investors with the promise of huge write-offs will largely vanish from the investment landscape.

Congress has mounted various assaults on tax shelters over the years in an attempt to curb abuses and prevent wealthy taxpayers from using them to completely escape paying taxes. But in drafting the new law Congress finally decided that a crippling blow was necessary if the new system was to be perceived as fair. The tax-shelter provisions are clearly one of the central features of the new tax system.

"The change is fundamental," said Senator Daniel Patrick Moynihan, Democrat of New York, who championed the tax-shelter provisions. "It is the greatest assault on tax shelters ever tried."

The assault comes on a number of fronts. The biggest blow is a provision that will no longer allow investors to use tax losses—the heart of traditional hard-core tax-shelter schemes—to offset their other income. Tax losses are created when the deductions produced by an investment exceed the income that the investment generates. The losses are often said to exist on paper only, in the sense that they do not represent an actual, out-of-pocket loss.

After a four-year phase-out, credits or deductions generated by a tax shelter can be used only to offset income produced by that tax shelter or by another shelter in which the individual has an interest. Any unused deductions can be carried forward to a future year to help offset future earnings of the shelter. But excess deductions cannot be used to offset the individual's wages, interest, dividends, stock market profits, or other such income. Only when the tax-shelter investment is sold or otherwise disposed of can the unused losses be claimed in full.

Many tax advisers are recommending that investors with large tax losses consider investing in a partnership that produces taxable income. By so doing, the tax losses, which might otherwise go to waste, could be used to shelter the income from the new partnership investment. The IRS intends to issue regulations that will delineate what kinds of activities qualify to offset the losses.

The new restrictions on tax losses primarily will affect the types of shelters that attracted people with six-figure incomes who were looking for big write-offs. These kinds of deals tended to be structured to maximize tax benefits and usually involved no more than thirty-five investors. These so-called "private placements" required the investor to put up a total of $20,000 to $150,000, often in installments over four or five years.

The new provision takes effect in 1987 but gives taxpayers who invested in a tax shelter before the new law was enacted a four-year phase-out. In 1987 65 percent of tax-shelter losses can still be claimed, in 1988 40 percent, in 1989 20 percent, and in 1990 10 percent. Some investors in low-income housing projects, who stood to be among the hardest hit by the new provision, were given more liberal transition relief.

To be sure, most tax-shelter investors who still have tax losses coming in are going to be hurt, particularly those who are paying in installments and were banking on the tax savings from the investment to help make those payments. The four-year phase-out will provide some cushion. But it won't help people who get hit by the alternative minimum tax. No tax losses are allowed in computing the minimum tax. Some tax-shelter syndicators are worried that a number of investors will simply walk away from the deal rather than make their remaining payments. Whether or not the investors can default will depend on the terms of the partnership agreement and debt obligations.

Trying to sell a partnership interest is no easy task. If you are able to find a buyer, you will likely receive only a fraction of its worth.

Deals where most of the tax benefits have already been realized may actually benefit from the new law. If the deal is starting to generate taxable income, the lower rates will provide a greater return.

AFFECTS "PASSIVE" INVESTORS IN ALL TYPES OF BUSINESSES

Except for real-estate developers and certain rental activities, the tax-shelter loss restrictions do not apply to people who actively run a trade or business. They will still be able to deduct more than they bring in from the business.

But the restrictions on tax-shelter losses do apply to people who put money into a small business and then play a largely "passive" role in its operation. The legislation indicates that a co-owner of, say, a flower shop or a restaurant would not be able to claim excess deductions on his tax return unless he had actively participated in the day-to-day operation of the business. The "passive" investor would be treated just like a tax-shelter investor and would not be allowed to use tax losses generated by the investment to offset taxes owed on his other income.

The restrictions apply to virtually any type of business arrangement where the investor's role in the operation is largely "passive." Taxpayers must be involved in the operations of the activity on a "regular, continuous,

133

and substantial basis" in order to claim the losses.

Periodic consultations with respect to general management decisions are not considered sufficient to meet the criterion. Nor does it matter whether the investor had full legal and financial responsibility for the enterprise.

As a result, the legislation indicates that a dentist who owns a flower shop with a brother who manages the operation full-time probably will not be able to claim any tax losses from the venture, even if the dentist helped make management decisions and filled in for his brother on vacations.

The New Trend in Tax Shelters

Tax-shelter promoters haven't been sitting by idly, watching their business die. They have been trying to restructure deals that are more in tune with the new tax rules. They are being designed more along the lines of the large "public" partnerships that attract smaller investors who put in as little as $2,000 to $5,000. These partnerships, which invest in everything from office buildings to motion pictures, are generally structured to generate income rather than tax losses.

In general, income-oriented deals will be helped by the reduction in individual tax rates. But part of their return does consist of tax benefits, which would be diminished in most cases under the new law.

For example, real-estate deals will be hurt by a cutback in depreciation deductions and the elimination of capital-gains tax treatment.

Further, the reduction in individual tax rates will diminish the value of all deductions and reduce the incentive for people to shelter income.

All of the changes in the tax-shelter area are likely to make investors reluctant to go into high-risk ventures, since the federal government will no longer help subsidize losses.

PHASE-IN OF NEW TAX-SHELTER LOSS LIMITATIONS

PERCENTAGE OF TAX-SHELTER LOSSES THAT CAN BE CLAIMED DURING PHASE-IN

Year	Percent Deductible
1987	65%
1988	40%
1989	20%
1990	10%
1991	0%

NOTE: The phase-in applies only to investments made before the legislation was enacted into law.

Oil- and Gas-Drilling Partnerships

Oil interests, which were well represented on the Senate tax-writing committee, won the one major exception to the restrictions on tax-shelter losses. Investors in a certain type of oil- and gas-drilling venture will be able to continue to use tax losses from the investment to offset their other income. The exception did not cover the typical oil and gas limited partnership. Rather the exception is provided only for arrangements in which the investors have a so-called "working interest" in the venture, which entails greater liability.

The exception will clearly give professionals an opportunity to shelter their income through an activity in which they play a mostly passive role. But it would also clearly require them to assume more risk than is usual.

Typically, the personal liability of tax-shelter investors is limited to the amount invested. These investors make no decisions or otherwise participate in the activity. But with a "working interest" in an oil and gas venture, investors could face additional financial exposure if problems develop, such as a well catching fire and causing injuries. Insurance might cover most contingencies, but investors would be personally liable if the coverage was insufficient.

In addition, the investors might be obligated to put up additional money if the cost of drilling proved higher than originally estimated.

They would also have some voice in deciding whether to put up more money to drill deeper. Nevertheless, their role would still largely remain a passive one.

Because of the extra liability investors have to assume, investment advisers recommend extreme caution. "You have to be very careful about the financial stability of the operator and the terms of the operating agreement," said Joel I. Berson, a partner in the New York law firm of Moore, Berson, Lifflander & Mewhinney.

In addition to the "working interest" exception, the oil industry was largely successful in retaining most of their tax benefits. Quick write-offs for intangible drilling costs were largely unchanged, except that integrated producers will have to amortize 30 percent of the costs over a five-year period. Drilling costs incurred overseas also are treated less favorably. Percentage depletion also is retained, except for payments made without regard to actual production, such as lease bonuses and advance royalties.

17

REAL-ESTATE
INVESTMENTS

Rental Housing

If you own a rental property—be it a condo, an apartment building, a house, or a vacation home—you still may be able to write off expenses in excess of the property's rental income. Landlords get a major exception to the tough restrictions on the use of tax-shelter losses. As a result, rental real estate will be one of the few tax shelters left.

Except for wealthier taxpayers, up to $25,000 a year in tax losses from rental properties can be used to offset your other income, including salary, interest, and dividends. The $25,000 cap is much more than most rental property owners have claimed in the past, so most owners should find the $25,000 limit more than sufficient. However, not everybody will be entitled to claim $25,000 in losses. The $25,000 allowance is reduced for people with adjusted gross incomes over $100,000 and completely eliminated for those with incomes above $150,000.

Being able to claim tax losses usually has meant the difference between making a profit and losing money on rental properties, since rental income alone is rarely enough to cover all expenses.

The $25,000 allowance isn't available for the typical limited partnership investment in real estate. Rather, to be eligible to claim tax losses, you have to "actively participate" in managing the property. That doesn't mean you necessarily have to be the stereotypical landlord who cleans the building and goes around the first of each month knocking on doors to collect the rent. It's enough if you make management decisions or arrange for others to provide services, such as repairs. Management decisions described in the congressional reports include "approving new tenants, deciding on rental terms, approving capital or repair expenditures, and other similar decisions."

Thus, the report said, someone who owns and rents out an apartment that was formerly his primary residence, or that he uses as a part-time vacation home, can be considered actively participating even if he hires a rental agent and others provide services, such as repairs.

You can own the rental property with other partners, but you can't own less than a 10-percent interest if you want to claim tax losses.

For people with adjusted gross incomes over $100,000, the $25,000 loss exception gets scaled back. It gets reduced by 50 cents for each dollar your income exceeds $100,000. So if your adjusted gross income is $125,000, you can deduct no more than $12,500 in losses. The loss exception is completely eliminated for people with adjusted gross incomes over $150,000. Consequently, wealthy taxpayers won't be able to claim tax losses except against income from other tax shelters or when the property is sold. As previously discussed, married couples living together will not be able to circumvent the income limitations by filing separate returns.

Even people whose principal business is real estate get bound by the limits.

Even if you are eligible to claim the tax losses, the value of the tax benefits are reduced in a variety of ways by the new law. First, the tax loss deductions will be worth far less because of the lower individual tax rates. If you were in the 40-percent tax bracket under the old law and had $10,000 in tax losses to claim, the tax savings would amount to $4,000. But under the new law, the same $10,000 in tax losses will provide only $2,800 in tax savings if your tax rate dropped to 28 percent.

Second, real estate becomes subject to the so-called "at-risk" rules, which generally limit the amount of tax-shelter losses you can claim to the amount you have invested or debts you are personally liable for. Real estate had been exempt from the "at-risk" rules under the old law, but the new law still allows an exception for real-estate loans made by financial institutions. So the new law mainly tightens the screws on seller-financed real estate.

To add salt to the wound, the amount of depreciation deductions you can claim each year will be reduced under the new law. The cost of residential real estate has to be written off over a period of twenty-seven and a half years using a straight-line formula. Commercial real estate has to be written off over thirty-one and a half years. Under the old law, which applies to real estate placed in service before January 1, 1987, the cost could be depreciated in nineteen years, using either a straight-line or an accelerated method that provided larger write-offs in the earlier years.

These changes will provide much smaller deductions each year. The new law will allow you to write off about 3.6 percent of the cost each year, compared to at least 5.3 percent under the old law. Investors who acquired real estate and placed it in service before January 1, 1987, will be allowed to continue to depreciate their properties over nineteen years.

The harsher tax rules obviously will reduce the return on many properties and turn some that were profitable under the old law into money-losing propositions. Higher rents would help close the gap, but market conditions and local rent-control laws can make it quite difficult to boost rents quickly. The prospect for higher rents is greater down the road because the reduced tax incentives are likely to lead to a slowdown in new apartment construction. Tighter housing supplies could also boost property values.

For rental properties that are profitable, the cutback in tax benefits will be offset by the reduction in individual tax rates, which means you will get to keep more of your profits.

Real estate, however, also loses the benefit of capital-gains tax treatment beginning in 1987. That will narrow your profits on the sale. However, people who acquired property in the past and used accelerated depreciation to write off the cost may not be hurt as much, if at all, since part of their sale profits was usually subject to regular tax rates rather than capital-gains rates.

The new law also limits the benefit of the installment-sale method for rental properties sold after August 16, 1986, for more than $150,000. Sales of under $150,000 were protected from the change, as were installment sales of such personal property as the family home.

Whether a rental property is still a good investment under the new law will depend on a variety of factors, including the rents being charged, the price of the property, operating expenses, and the value of the tax benefits. The only way to determine the bottom line is to make the calculations. "There's no substitute for what I call pushing the pencil," said Herbert Paul, a New York tax attorney.

Rehabilitation Projects and Low-Income Housing Investments

Investors in low-income housing projects and older building renovations are also eligible to use tax credits earned from those projects to offset tax on up to $25,000 of other income. You don't even have to "actively participate" in either of these projects to qualify. It can be a limited partnership venture where you simply put in your money and sit back and wait for the general partner to mail you your checks and notify you about how many tax credits you earned each year. Further, the income guidelines for the credit exception are even more liberal than for the landlord exception. Investors with adjusted gross incomes of up to $200,000 are allowed the full $25,000 exception. The amount is gradually reduced for incomes above $200,000 and completely eliminated for incomes above $250,000.

Tax credits for the costs of rehabilitating older buildings were retained by the new law, but in reduced and modified form. For certified historic structures, the credit drops to 20 percent, from 25 percent under the old law. For nonhistoric buildings that were originally built before 1936, the credit is 10 percent. The old law provided a 20-percent credit for buildings more than forty years old and a 15-percent credit for buildings more than thirty years old.

The new law applies to property placed in service after 1986. As was the case under the old law, certified historic structures can be either residential or nonresidential property. But the nonhistoric buildings have to be nonresidential.

The new law creates a new tax credit for investments in low-income housing, replacing a variety of incentives available under the old law. Only these new credits qualify for the $25,000 exception. The credits range from 4 percent to 9 percent of expenditures and can be claimed annually for ten years. The 9-percent credit applies to new construction or rehabilitation of low-income units that are not financed with tax-exempt bonds or other federal subsidies. The 4-percent credit applies to subsidized projects or the acquisition of low-income housing units.

The credits are generally available for property placed in service or acquired after 1986 and before 1990.

18

FRINGE BENEFITS AND EXECUTIVE PERKS

Tax-free Status of Fringe Benefits

The new law retains the tax-free status of virtually all of the popular fringe benefits that employees commonly receive, including company-paid health plans and the first $50,000 of group term life insurance coverage.

But Congress decided to impose new "nondiscrimination" rules to health- and life-insurance plans to prevent employers from showering higher-paid executives with these tax-free benefits while giving lower-paid workers little or none. To the extent the new rules are not complied with, higher-paid workers may find part or all of their benefits are subject to tax, even though any lower-paid workers covered under the plan would continue to receive the benefits tax-free.

Companies generally have a year or two to comply with the new guidelines. Some employers may well expand their coverage to include more lower-paid and part-time workers in order to protect the tax-free status of fringe benefits for higher-paid workers. But other companies might find this approach too costly and simply let the higher-paid workers be subject to tax on their benefits. Many of these employers might beef up their executives' salaries enough to help offset the tax.

Otherwise, Congress tiptoed around the sacred turf of fringe benefits and made few changes. Lawmakers even extended the tax-free status of a few special benefits whose tax exemptions were set to expire under the old law.

GROUP LEGAL SERVICE PLANS: The tax exclusion for company-sponsored plans that provide legal services to employees and their families is extended through the end of 1987. Their tax-free status was originally scheduled to expire at the end of 1985.

EMPLOYER-PROVIDED EDUCATIONAL ASSISTANCE: Employees will be able to exclude from income the first $5,250 they receive under educational assistance programs at work for tuition, fees, books, supplies, and the like. That $5,250 cap, which is effective beginning in 1986, was increased from $5,000 under the old law. The exclusion was originally scheduled to expire at the end of 1985. The new law extends the exclusion only through the end of 1987.

DEPENDENT-CARE ASSISTANCE PLANS: The new law limits to $5,000 a year the value of employer-provided child-care services that an employee can exclude from tax. (The limit is $2,500 for a married person filing a separate return.) Previously, there was no overall cap on the value of benefits that could be excluded from the employee's income. The new cap is effective beginning in 1987.

Congress, however, took away the tax-free status of employer-provided commuter van pools. The exemption for this transportation service that some companies provided as a convenience to their employees expired at the end of 1985. The new law did not revive the exemption.

Employee Awards

Employees who are honored by their employer with an achievement award may get a gift from the federal government as well. Employees receiving length-of-service or safety-achievement awards will generally not have to pay tax on the gift so long as it is a gift of property, such as a gold watch, rather than cash or gift certificates. The tax exclusion is generally limited to gifts of $400, but can be as high as $1,600, depending on the kind of award program the employer has. If you receive an award, first thank your employer for the honor and then ask him about the tax treatment of the gift. Any amounts that are not tax-free will routinely be included by your employer on your W-2 form.

The new tax law also retains the tax-free status of employer gifts of small value—so-called de-minimus fringe benefits—such as Christmas turkeys or hams given to employees.

Faculty Members and Campus Housing

Faculty members who live in campus housing and pay the college little or no rent will have to pay tax on part of the benefit. The provision follows years of disagreement between the Internal Revenue Service and educational institutions over the tax treatment of campus housing. Several court decisions have held that the rental value of school-furnished housing is not a tax-free benefit for faculty members.

To determine how much, if any, of the benefit is taxable to the faculty member, the new law sets the annual fair-market rent at 5 percent of the appraised value of the lodging. If the faculty member pays at least that amount in rent, then no tax is due.

For example, if a house is valued at $80,000, the fair-market rent would be $333.33 a month, or $4,000 a year (5 percent x $80,000). If the faculty member paid the college at least $4,000 a year in rent, none of the benefit is taxable. But if only $3,000 a year in rent was paid, the faculty member would have to include $1,000 ($4,000 − $3,000) in income for tax purposes.

Even with the tax, faculty members are likely to find that campus lodging is still a pretty good deal compared with private off-campus housing in many college towns.

The provision was effective beginning in 1986.

Executive Compensation and Incentive Stock Options

Executives will find that incentive stock options and other forms of deferred compensation lose some of their appeal under the new law.

Gains from incentive stock options will be taxed more harshly with the repeal of preferential long-term capital-gains treatment. At the same time, the reduction in individual tax rates reduces the benefit of deferred compensation schemes.

Nonetheless, stock options are likely to remain an important part of executive compensation packages. And deferred compensation plans are likely to offer a popular way to defer income until tax rates are fully lowered in 1988, even though their appeal may subside after that.

INCENTIVE STOCK OPTIONS

From Silicon Valley in California to the executive suites in Manhattan, incentive stock options have been a popular way for companies to attract and retain executive talent, giving executives a way to profit handsomely if the company and its stock performs well. Of course, this gives the executive the incentive to perform well so that the price of the stock rises. Incentive stock options have been particularly valuable to small start-up companies that can't afford to lure executive talent with big salaries. Instead, these companies can offer executives a chance to prosper if the company prospers.

With an incentive stock option, the executive has the right to buy a certain number of shares of stock at a set price over a period of years. Most options last ten years. If the stock rises sharply, the executive can "exercise" the option and buy the stock at the lower price set by the option. For instance, if your company gave you an option to buy stock at $10 a share and it rose to $50, you could exercise the option and buy the stock at $10, for a $40 gain.

To add to the attraction, gains on the stock option wouldn't be taxed until you actually sold the stock. And then you would be taxed at favorable capital-gains tax rates—provided you complied with certain holding period requirements.

Incentive stock options would become less attractive under the new law because of the repeal of capital-gains treatment. The new law still allows you to defer taxes on incentive stock options until you sell the stock, although the gain at the time of exercise remains subject to the alternative minimum tax. But the new law generally encourages most people to exercise the option and sell their stock at the same time.

But taxes are but one part of the allure of incentive stock options. They can provide big rewards if the company's stock appreciates.

And although the new law means a bigger tax bite, incentive stock options will be more flexible for executives. Since long-term capital-gains tax treatment will be eliminated, executives don't have to worry about complying with the special holding periods after 1987.

Until the end of 1987, the holding period will remain important because long-term capital gains will still be treated more favorably than other income. In 1987, long-term gains will be taxed at a maximum 28 percent rate while other income will be taxed as high as 38.5 percent. Thus, if the stock is sold before the special holding-period requirements for incentive stock options are met, profits will be taxed at rates as high as 38.5 percent. So to ensure that profits are taxed at no more than 28 percent, the two holding-period requirements for incentive stock options have to be met: The stock has to be held at least two years from the date the option was originally granted, and for at least one year beyond the date on which the option was exercised and the stock was purchased.

After 1987 the special holding periods would be irrelevant (except if you have other capital losses that need offsetting), since failure to heed them would simply mean that profits would be taxed as ordinary income at rates of 15 and 28 percent (33 percent if you count the hidden rate). That is the same fate that would befall someone who followed the holding period.

But that is not the end of the story. There may even be a benefit to be gained by violating the holding period. If you are thinking of selling the stock before the holding period is up, you might be able to make a deal with your boss. Why would the boss be willing to deal? Well, the company stands to make some money if you violate the holding period.

The rules, which were not changed by the new law, entitle the company to claim a tax deduction for granting an incentive stock option if the executive violates the holding period. In the past, companies rarely got the deduction, since most executives wanted to take advantage of the capital-gains treatment and thus complied with the holding-period requirements.

But beginning in 1988 an executive will be taxed the same whether the holding period is met or not. So executives might be able to do a little horse-trading with their boss. "It puts the executive in the driver's seat," said Peter Elinsky, a tax partner at the accounting firm of Peat Marwick. The executive, he said, might be able to work a deal where he would agree to sell the stock before the holding period is up if the company agreed to pass on some of the benefit of the tax deduction it would get.

The new law would also encourage people to exercise the option and sell the stock at the same time, Mr. Elinsky said. Since the holding-period requirements would be moot, there would no longer be reason for the executive to wait before selling the stock. The exception would be executives who are bound by Securities and Exchange Commission rules relating to corporate "insiders" and have to wait before selling their shares. Another exception would be an executive who has an option about to expire and thus needs to exercise the option right away, but is not yet ready to sell the stock.

The changes in the tax treatment of incentive stock options may prompt companies to consider another type of stock option for their executives, so-called nonqualified options. Executives would have to pay tax on the gain when they exercise the option, which would be of no harm if they sell the stock at the same time. Meanwhile, companies are assured of getting a tax deduction when the options are exercised, a benefit they don't always get with incentive stock options.

OTHER CHANGES IN INCENTIVE STOCK OPTIONS

For incentive stock options issued after 1986, the new law eliminates the requirement that you have to exercise stock options in the order they were granted. That requirement used to pose a problem for executives at companies whose stock price had fallen. Now, if your company's stock price falls below the exercise price of your option, your company might well issue a second option with a lower exercise price. You will be allowed to exercise the second option first instead of having to wait for the stock to rebound above the first option's exercise price. Options issued before 1987, however, must still be exercised in the order granted.

The new law also liberalized the $100,000 limit on incentive stock options that a company could grant an employee in any one year. Instead, the $100,000 limit applies to the amount that become first exercisable in any one calendar year. Thus, a company could issue an executive more than $100,000 in any one year so long as no more than $100,000 is set to be first allowed to be exercisable in any one year.

DEFERRED COMPENSATION PLANS

With tax rates dropping, many executives may start favoring cash to deferred compensation. Deferred compensation plans have long been popular among executives who faced high tax rates. They sought to defer much of their compensation, often until they retired when they would be in a lower tax bracket. But with tax rates sharply reduced, many executives will not find themselves in a lower bracket on retirement. In fact, many of them worry that Congress will eventually be forced to push tax rates back up. So if they elect to defer income, executives fear they will be deferring it to a time when it will be taxed at a higher rate, rather than a lower one. As a result, many compensation experts predict that executives will be asking for bigger salaries instead of bigger deferred benefits. Before that happens, deferred compensation plans are likely to be especially popular in 1986 and 1987 as executives try to defer income until tax rates are fully reduced.

19

RETIREMENT PLANS

The new law makes sweeping changes to employer-sponsored retirement plans. Many of the provisions are intended to increase coverage for lower- and middle-income workers and prevent higher-paid workers and executives from drawing too much of a benefit from tax-favored plans.

Companies will be busy trying to figure out how to adjust their retirement programs to the new law. "Thousands of plans are going to be disqualified," said Harold Dankner, a partner and employee compensation specialist at the accounting firm of Coopers & Lybrand. As a result, many companies will need to make substantial changes to their pension plans in order to retain their tax-favored status.

The decisions will be tough. Employers will be weighing whether to simply absorb the added cost of increasing benefits and broadening coverage for rank-and-file workers, or to reduce the benefits for others in order to contain costs.

The new law will also limit the amount of salary that higher-paid workers can put into tax-favored retirement plans. And the rules limit the amount that can be paid out of company pension plans to executives who retire early.

In addition, the new law makes changes intended to discourage people from withdrawing money from pension plans early and using the funds for something other than their original purpose, which is retirement. Even those who withdraw funds on retirement will find the tax treatment is not as generous as it used to be.

Despite the many changes, the new law retains, and in some cases expands upon, the benefits of employer retirement plans. Workers will generally earn rights to a pension benefit after five years on the job, about half the time it took under the old law. And employers who take Social Security benefits into account in determining the level of pension benefits an employee gets will no longer be able to reduce the private benefit down to little or nothing. The new law also largely retains the favorable tax treatment of Employee Stock Ownership Plans, which are employer plans that invest primarily in the company's own securities.

Earlier Pension Benefits

American workers will earn rights to pension benefits much sooner under the new tax law. Most people have had to work ten years for a company before they established full rights to benefits that had accrued on their behalf from employer contributions into the pension plan. If the employee left the company before completing ten years of service, he typically left without a cent in pension benefits. Any benefits that had accrued on his behalf were simply forfeited because he was not yet "vested."

The new law will require employers to sharply reduce the "vesting" period—the time frame under which the employee acquires the nonforfeitable right to employer-contributed benefits.

Employers have the choice of two vesting schedules. One option, known as "cliff" vesting, will require that employees be 100 percent vested after completing five years of service. The other option, known as "graded" vesting, requires the employee to have the nonforfeitable right to at least 20 percent of his or her accrued benefit after three years of service, 40 percent at the end of four years, 60 percent at the end of five years, 80 percent at the end of six years, and 100 percent at the end of seven years of service.

This vesting provision is one of the most far-reaching changes to be found in the new tax law and will have a significant impact on millions of workers. The change will be especially helpful to people who tend to shift jobs frequently and don't stay long enough to acquire the right to a pension benefit.

The new vesting schedule will not make company loyalty a thing of the past. Someone who leaves the job after five years will still receive a smaller benefit than a worker who stayed at the company ten years. The difference under the new law is that the person who leaves after five years will no longer leave empty-handed.

Of course, the quicker vesting will make pension plans a more expensive proposition for employers. Some pension experts raised concerns that the new requirements could have a chilling effect and might discourage some employers, particularly smaller businesses, from setting up new plans for their employees, or from maintaining their existing plans. Another concern is that some employers might reduce the level of benefits for longer-term employees in order to pay the new costs of providing benefits for shorter-term employees. However, most companies are expected to foot the extra bill because pension plans are a major attraction for employees.

Employers have a couple of years during which to make the transition. The new vesting rules generally do not go into effect until 1989. At that point, both new and existing participants in the plan will be covered by the new vesting schedules.

The accelerated vesting requirements, however, will not apply to multiemployer plans—those cosponsored by a number of companies within a particular industry. These plans, which are common in unionized industries, would need to offer only ten-year vesting.

"Integrated" Plans

Many workers who are covered by a type of company pension plan that takes their Social Security benefits into account in determining their retirement pay are likely to receive a much larger pension under the new law.

Companies that link the size of pension payouts to the employee's Social Security benefits will no longer be able to reduce pension benefits by more than 50 percent. The pension plans affected are referred to as "integrated" plans because Social Security benefits are integrated with the level of pension benefits.

Under the old law, many lower-paid workers never got a cent in private pension because companies were allowed to reduce the employee's pension entitlement by a substantial portion of their Social Security benefits. Typically, the law permitted employers to reduce the pension payment by up to $83\frac{1}{3}$ percent of the expected Social Security benefit. In many cases, that was enough to wipe out the pension benefit. For example, if an employee were promised a $5,000-a-year pension and received $6,500 a year in Social Security, he would receive no private pension benefit.

Under the new law, private pension benefits generally cannot be reduced by more than 50 percent. So the employee would receive at least $2,500 in pension benefits on top of the Social Security.

Lawmakers thought the old formula that allowed employers to eliminate any pension benefit for lower-paid workers undermined the original congressional intent for providing tax incentives for pension plans—i.e., to encourage employers to provide workers with retirement benefits to augment Social Security.

Employers are given some time to make the transition. The new rule does not go into effect until 1989.

Government Workers Lose Tax-free Retirement Period

Government workers and some employees in the private sector will no longer receive special tax treatment when they retire and start receiving payments from their retirement annuities. They will have to start paying taxes on part of their pension checks immediately.

Under the old law, retirees didn't have to pay taxes on their pension income for up to three years after they retired. The reason: The law treated these early payouts as being drawn solely from contributions employees made to the plan with their after-tax dollars. Those payouts, which could last up to three years but typically lasted about eighteen months, weren't subject to tax on withdrawal. This was known as the three-year-basis recovery rule. When the employee's contributions were exhausted, pension checks became fully taxable, since the disbursements were then being drawn on employer contributions.

Under the new law, retirees will no longer have a tax-free period. From the start, pension checks will be treated as being drawn partly from personal contributions and partly from employer contributions. So a large portion of each pension check will be taxable and a small portion will be non-taxable. Rather than recovering personal contributions up front, they will be recovered a bit at a time over the rest of the retiree's life.

Theoretically, this will not increase the total amount of taxes that employees will have to pay on their benefits. But it will make them start paying taxes earlier on their pension income.

Many retirees used to take advantage of that tax-free period to sell some investments. Since their pension checks were tax-free, they would be in a low tax bracket and profits from the sale of the investments would be taxed at lower rates. Retirees won't have the same opportunity under the new law, although the reduction in individual tax rates should help offset the loss of the tax-free period.

The change affects only individuals who retire after July 1, 1986. Technically, the cutoff applies to individuals whose "annuity starting date" is after July 1, 1986.

The changes will affect millions of federal, state, and local government workers. Many employees in the private sector who receive payouts from company thrift plans will also be affected by the change in rules.

Tax-Sheltered Annuities for Teachers and Others

Teachers and workers at religious and certain other tax-exempt organizations are often given the opportunity to participate in retirement plan programs in which part of their salary can be contributed to purchase a tax-sheltered annuity contract. As with a 401(k) plan, the portion of their salary contributed to a tax-sheltered annuity is not subject to immediate tax. Taxes are deferred until the retirement payments are received. These plans are often referred to as 403(b) plans, for the section of the tax code where they are described.

Beginning in 1987 the maximum amount that an employee can earmark is $9,500 a year, compared to $30,000 under the old law. The $9,500 cap will be adjusted for inflation each year starting when the $7,000 cap on 401(k) plans reaches $9,500. That is not likely to occur for several years. Only a small portion of workers ever put more than $9,500 a year into the plan anyway.

The new law also applies some new nondiscrimination requirements on employers to encourage them to provide retirement plan coverage to more lower-paid workers.

Withdrawal Penalties

Withdrawing money early from a retirement plan, if your employer allows it, will become a more expensive proposition under the new law.

The same 10-percent penalty that has long applied to early withdrawals from Individual Retirement Accounts is extended under the new law to most other retirement plans, including tax-sheltered annuities, beginning in 1987. That means that if you withdraw money before age fifty-nine and a half, become disabled, or die, you will generally have to pay a 10-percent penalty on taxable amounts withdrawn on top of any regular taxes due.

There are a few exceptions. Among them are:
1) if you take early retirement, are at least fifty-five years old, and meet requirements for early retirement under the plan;
2) if the money is used to pay medical expenses to the extent they are deductible;
3) if the distribution is part of a scheduled series of equal periodic payments to stretch over the remainder of your life (generally restricted to distributions after separation from service);
4) distributions from employee stock ownership plans prior to 1990;
5) certain payments made pursuant to a domestic-relations order; and
6) lump-sum distributions made prior to March 15, 1987, if the distribution is made on account of separation from service in 1986 and you treat the distribution for federal tax purposes as paid in 1986.

Amounts distributed from unfunded deferred compensation plans of tax-exempt organizations or state and local governments are exempt from the penalty.

HARDSHIP WITHDRAWAL RESTRICTIONS
The new law also restricts hardship withdrawals from 401(k)s and tax-sheltered annuities to contributions made by the employee, but not earnings on that income. This restriction applies after December 31, 1988.

CHECK THE RULES WITH YOUR EMPLOYER
Check the restrictions and penalties on withdrawals with your pension-plan administrator or your tax adviser before making any withdrawals. Also check with your plan administrator to find out exactly how much you are allowed to contribute and how much you can expect to get at retirement. For elderly workers who are in no hurry to retire or get at their retirement funds, be aware that the new law sets a uniform maximum age for when individuals must start receiving distributions from their retirement plans. Withdrawals must begin no later than April 1 following the year you reach age seventy and a half—regardless of whether you are still working. The new rules take effect after 1988. An exception was made for employees (other than 5 percent or more owners of the business) who reach age seventy and a half by January 1, 1988. They can defer distributions until they retire, if they desire.

Lump-Sum Pension Payment

If you receive a lump-sum distribution from a pension or profit-sharing plan, you have a couple of choices as to what to do with it. You can take the money and pay tax on it. Or you can roll it over into an IRA, where you can defer paying taxes on the money.

If you are moving to another job, you may have the third option of rolling the money over into your new employer's pension plan (if your new employer allows it) and deferring taxes on it.

ROLLING IT OVER INTO AN IRA

The new law retains the IRA rollover option. If you don't need all the funds from your pension distribution for a while, the IRA rollover offers you the advantage of being able to defer taxes on the money and letting it grow and compound in a tax-free environment.

The normal $2,000-a-year contribution limit to IRAs doesn't apply when you're making a rollover. There is no limit on the amount you can deposit. Nor do you get a deduction for depositing the lump-sum payment into the IRA. Otherwise, the rollover IRA works just like a regular IRA. Money in the account escapes the clutches of the IRS until it's withdrawn.

TAKING THE MONEY AND PAYING TAX IMMEDIATELY

If, instead, you decide to simply take the lump-sum payment in hand and do with it as you please, you will have to pay tax on it immediately. But the tax law provides a special formula for computing tax on lump-sum payments that eases the bite.

For the taxable portion of your distribution that represents the time you were in the pension plan before 1974, you were allowed capital-gains tax treatment under the old law.

For the portion representing your time in the plan from 1974 on, the old law allowed a ten-year income-averaging method for taxing lump sums. Although all the money is taxed at once, it is taxed as if you had received it evenly over ten years. The bottom line is that the tax bite is much smaller.

The new law phases out the capital-gains treatment over a six-year period and scales back ten-year averaging to five-year income averaging. The switch from ten-year to five-year averaging might seem like a harsh change, but the impact is mitigated by the new tax rate system. "While five years isn't as good as ten years, the rates are lower," said Leon M. Nad, associate vice chairman of taxes at the accounting firm of Price Waterhouse.

Under the new law, the five-year averaging and capital-gains tax treatment is generally allowed only for a single lump-sum distribution received after you reach age fifty-nine and a half. So if you have lump-sum distributions coming from more than one employer, you should consider the most advantageous use of the special tax treatment.

SPECIAL PROTECTIONS FOR PEOPLE OVER AGE FIFTY

While the provisions take effect beginning in 1987, Congress provided some special transition rules for people who reached age fifty before January 1, 1986. If you fall into that category, you will pretty much be protected from the tax changes.

First, you can take advantage of the capital-gains tax treatment for the pre-1974 portion of your lump-sum payment without regard to the six-year phase-out. The money will be taxed at a straight 20 percent, regardless of your tax bracket.

Second, you have the choice of using either the new five-year averaging formula under the new lower tax rate schedule, or you can stick with the ten-year formula using the higher tax rates that were in effect for 1986. You will have to make the calculation to determine which method is more beneficial for you.

Third, you can use the special tax treatment for a lump-sum payment received either before or after you reach age fifty-nine and a half. But you have only one chance to use the special treatment. So if you have more than one lump-sum distribution coming, you'll have to decide which one you want the special treatment to apply to.

EVALUATING THE OPTIONS

There's no one answer on whether to roll the money over into an IRA or have the money taxed immediately using the favorable income-averaging formula and capital-gains treatment. Of course, if you aren't eligible for the special tax treatment, the IRA becomes especially attractive. But if you do have the choice, you'll need to make some comparisons. "You've got to do some calculations," said Sidney Kess, national director of tax policy at the accounting firm of KMG Main Hurdman.

The decision will hinge largely on when you need the money. If you don't need the money right away, determine how many years it will be before you need it and whether the benefit of having it grow and compound tax-free in an IRA will more than offset the higher tax you may have to pay when the money is withdrawn from the IRA. (If you choose to roll the lump sum into an IRA, you don't get any special tax treatment when you withdraw the money later.)

As a rule of thumb, you should stay away from an IRA if you expect to need the money shortly after you put it in, because the money withdrawn will be taxed at regular rates. But if you don't need all the money right away and you don't have a large pre-1974 distribution, Andrew Zuckerman of Arthur Andersen says individuals will usually be better off rolling the money into an IRA and drawing it out over a period of time as needed.

Don't forget that you may also have the option of receiving monthly pension checks from your employer instead of taking a lump-sum payment. The change in tax rules may provide an incentive for people to compare the advantages of each more closely. "There's no substitution for laying out all the options and running through the calculations," said Harold Dankner of Coopers & Lybrand.

Highly Paid Executives Face New Restrictions

Executives who retire early will find the benefits they are allowed to receive from defined benefit pension plans are sharply reduced.

The new law retains the maximum $90,000-a-year cap for people who retire at the usual retirement age, which is now age sixty-five. And the limits will be indexed for inflation so that benefits can keep up with the cost of living. But the new law reduces the limit for people who retire before they reach social security retirement age, which is now sixty-five, but increases to age sixty-six for those born between 1938 and 1954, and age sixty-seven for those born after 1954.

These actuarial reductions can be substantial. Under the old law, for instance, the $90,000 benefit could be paid to people retiring as early as age sixty-two. But the new law would reduce that to $72,000, based on certain actuarial assumptions, for people born before 1938. For people born between 1938 and 1954, the limit would be about $67,500; and, for people born after 1954, $63,000.

The cuts are even more dramatic for people who retire at age fifty-five.

The old law allowed them as much as a $75,000 benefit. But the new law reduces that to less than $40,000 for those born before 1938; to about $37,400 for people born between 1938 through 1954; and less than $35,000 for people born after 1954.

Previously accrued benefits are protected. So an executive who is sixty-two and accrued a $90,000 benefit would still be able to get the $90,000 benefit if he retired early. But a fifty-year-old executive who planned to retire at age fifty-five and had benefits accrued up to the new limits would be bound by the new limits.

The new law also proportionately reduces the maximum benefit for people who have participated in the plan for less than ten years.

Many top executives will not be hurt by the changes. Most large companies have so-called unfunded plans from which supplemental benefits can be paid to executives. These unfunded plans don't fall under the same tough restrictions as tax-favored pension plans, so they have long been used to supplement the retirement benefits of key executives. Because of the new restrictions on early retirement benefits, these unfunded plans are likely to be relied on much more.

"The limitations are becoming so severe that I think more and more executives are going to be looking to supplemental arrangements to protect their income," said Everett T. Allen, vice president at Towers, Perrin Forster & Crosby, a benefits consulting firm. The problem is that these supplemental arrangements are unsecured promises of the corporation. In other words, these benefits aren't guaranteed in the event the company runs into trouble. Another problem is not all executives get covered by these supplemental plans.

As a result, executives may well become more interested in creating some added income security by asking their employers for greater current compensation, which they can invest on their own for retirement.

Tax-exempt organizations and government employees are exempt from the actuarial reduction provision. Special rules also apply to police and firefighters.

For commercial airline pilots, the normal retirement age is sixty for purposes of determining the maximum allowed benefit limit.

EXCESS BENEFITS TAX

Highly paid corporate executives will also run up against a new excise tax when they withdraw very large amounts from tax-favored retirement plans in a single year, including IRAs. The 15-percent excise tax is imposed on distributions in excess of $112,500 in one year. Lump-sum distributions are subject to a separate limitation of $562,500. The excise tax applies only to the amount in excess of those sums.

The tax does not apply to distributions that are rolled over to an IRA or another qualified plan, or are attributable to after-tax employee contributions. Special rules also partly exempt benefits accrued before August 2, 1986.

Unfunded Deferred Compensation Arrangements for State and Local Governments and Tax-Exempts

Restrictions on the deferred compensation plans, which have been offered to employees of state and local governments, will also apply to employees of tax-exempt organizations as well beginning in 1987. Such plans generally allow deferrals of the lesser of $7,500 or 33$^{1}/_{3}$ percent of compensation—net of the deferral.

The maximum amount has to be reduced dollar-for-dollar for elective contributions made by the employee to tax-sheltered annuities, Simplified Employee Pension Plans, and 401(k) plans.

Simplified Employee Pension Plans (SEPs)

Owners of small businesses who want to set up a retirement plan that is simple to administer and allows employees to make their own voluntary contributions to it—as with a 401(k) plan—may find that Simplified Employee Pension Plans (SEPs) fit the bill.

SEPs were created by Congress in 1978 to help small businesses set up pension plans for themselves and their employees without having to go through the administrative paperwork of traditional pension plans. To date, relatively few small businesses have taken advantage of SEPs. But the new tax law may make them a more popular option, at least for companies with twenty-five or fewer employees. These plans not only will be relatively simple to set up but they will also combine the features of a pension plan and a 401(k) plan.

The old law allowed only the employer to contribute money to an SEP on behalf of his employees. But beginning in 1987 the new law will also permit employees to voluntarily contribute part of their pre-tax salaries to the

SEP as if they were making contributions to a 401(k) plan. The same $7,000-a-year limit that applies to 401(k)s applies to employee contributions to SEPs. The option, however, is available only if the company has twenty-five or fewer employees and at least half of the employees elect to make such contributions.

Taxation of Social Security Benefits

Elderly taxpayers will find the new tax law did not change the formula for determining how much, if any, of their Social Security benefits are subject to tax. The vast majority of Social Security recipients will continue to receive their benefits tax-free.

But some recipients will discover that more of their Social Security benefits are subject to tax because of a few indirect changes produced by the new law. Some retirees could find their benefits vulnerable to tax for the first time because of the new law. People affected by this should not necessarily be alarmed. Their total tax bill might very well still end up lower under the new law because of the lower tax rates.

As has been the case since 1984, middle- and upper-income retirees face paying tax on part of their Social Security benefits if their income exceeds $32,000 on a joint return and $25,000 for single persons. For purposes of this threshold test, income is defined as adjusted gross income plus tax-exempt interest and half of your Social Security benefits. If your income tops those base amounts of $32,000 or $25,000, then you have to include in taxable income either the amount by which your income exceeds the base figure or half of your Social Security benefits, whichever is less. In other words, you never have to pay tax on more than half of your Social Security benefits.

Although this formula is not changed, adjusted gross income will become a larger figure for some taxpayers. The reason is that the new law will expose more income to tax. For example, the old 60-percent tax exclusion for long-term capital gains will be eliminated. So will the exclusion for the first $200 in stock dividends received ($100 for single individuals).

With those exclusions gone, adjusted gross income will go up for taxpayers with dividend or capital-gains income, resulting in more of their Social Security benefits being subject to tax. But, again, for many retirees, this increase in the amount of Social Security benefits that has to be exposed to tax will likely be offset by the lower tax rates.

20

UPPER-INCOME TAXPAYERS AND THE ALTERNATIVE MINIMUM TAX

Since Congress was reluctant to make a wholesale cleanup of special tax breaks, some opportunities might appear to remain for individuals to whittle their tax bill down to little or nothing. But the new law contains a trapdoor. It is a fairly potent "alternative minimum tax" that will render many tax preferences impotent and insure that almost no wealthy individual escapes paying a minimum amount of taxes.

In essence, the alternative minimum tax is a shadow tax system. If individuals take advantage of too many special tax breaks—bringing their regular tax bill down too far—the alternative minimum tax takes over and reinflates that tax bill. Taxpayers calculate their tax liability first under the conventional method and then under the alternative tax method. They pay whichever tax is higher.

Most taxpayers are generally shielded from the alternative minimum tax because of a $40,000 exemption on joint returns; $30,000 for individuals; and $20,000 for married persons filing separate returns.

By itself, the alternative tax resembles in many respects the simple tax system that many people envisioned when President Reagan first broached the idea of restructuring the tax system. Many of the deductions and preferences that are allowed in computing regular tax liability, such as the state and local tax deduction, are disallowed when computing the alternative minimum tax. Individuals can generally deduct only charitable contributions, mortgage interest, other interest up to the amount of net investment income; gambling losses; casualty and theft losses; and medical deductions in excess of 10 percent of adjusted gross income.

A minimum tax in one form or another has been part of the tax code since 1969. The new minimum tax is somewhat tougher than the old minimum tax because the rate is slightly higher and the range of tax preferences that must be added back to income has been expanded. Beginning in 1987, the rate is raised from 20 percent to 21 percent, which is still much lower than the top regular tax rate. But the 21 percent rate is assessed on a broader base of income. Byrle Abbin, managing director of federal tax services at the accounting firm of Arthur Andersen & Company, believes one reason more wealthy people may be vulnerable to the new minimum tax is that the difference between the regular rate and the alternative minimum tax rate has narrowed so much.

Another reason is that the $40,000 exemption ($30,000 for single individuals) is phased out for wealthier individuals. When income is computed under the minimum tax formula, the exemption is reduced by 25 cents for each dollar that income exceeds $150,000 on joint returns; $112,500 for individuals; and $75,000 for married persons filing separately. The entire exemption disappears once income reaches $310,000 on a joint return; $232,500 for individuals; and $155,000 for married persons filing separately.

However, many stock market investors who found themselves hit by the alternative minimum tax under the old law because they had large capital gains will no longer be burdened by the alternative tax. Because preferential treatment of long-term capital gains is eliminated under the regular tax, it no longer is included in the minimum tax computation.

People who make large charitable gifts of stock, artwork, land, or other appreciated property become vulnerable to the minimum tax. Beginning in 1987, a portion of the charitable deduction for contributions of appreciated property becomes a preference item in the minimum tax computation. The portion included is the net appreciation of the property. For example, assume you purchased stock for $10 a share and it subsequently rose to $50 a share, at which time you gave it to charity. The $40 gain, which you do not have to pay regular tax on if you give the stock to charity, is the preference amount that gets included in the minimum tax computation. The preference doesn't apply to carryforwards of contributions made before August 16, 1986.

Another new preference item is tax-exempt interest on certain private-purpose bonds issued after August 7, 1986. This category mainly includes industrial development bonds, student loan bonds, and housing bonds.

Other municipal bonds are not subject to the tax, making the alternative tax less than foolproof.

Tax shelter investors, however, may well get caught by the alternative tax. From 1987 through 1990, tax shelter investors will still be allowed to claim some tax losses in computing their regular tax liability. In 1987, for instance, 65 percent of tax shelter losses can be claimed. But the losses that can be claimed under the regular tax during the phase-out period have to be added back to income in computing the alternative minimum tax. In other words, the minimum tax does not give a transition period before tax shelter losses are disallowed. Largely because of this, the alternative minimum tax may well remain a significant threat to many upper-income individuals over the next few years. By 1991, when tax shelter losses can no longer be used to offset other income in the regular tax, these losses will mean nothing in terms of the alternative minimum tax. As a result of this, along with the repeal of capital-gains treatment for regular tax purposes, the alternative tax will likely become relatively insignificant to most individuals. In other words, the regular tax itself will prevent people from escaping without paying a minimum amount of taxes.

Among other preferences subject to the minimum tax are passive farming losses, certain income deferred from the use of the "completed-contract" method of accounting for long-term contracts, and income deferred from the installment method of accounting for dispositions of certain business property and sales of rental property where the sales price exceeds $150,000.

Most of the preference items from the old law were also retained with some modifications, including accelerated depreciation; intangible drilling costs to the extent they exceed 65 percent of net income from oil, gas, and geothermal properties; expensing of mining exploration and development costs; expensing of circulation expenditures for newspapers and magazines; expensing of research and experimentation expenditures; and percentage depletion.

When you exercise an incentive stock option, the excess of the fair market value of stock over the exercise price of the option is a preference.

Under the new law, the foreign tax credit cannot be used to offset more than 90 percent of the minimum tax.

Be aware that the deduction for mortgage interest allowed in the minimum tax computation can be less than allowed for the regular tax. If a mortgage loan is refinanced for more than its immediately prior outstanding balance, the deduction for minimum tax purposes is limited to the prior outstanding balance. Futhermore, the minimum tax limits the mortgage deduction to amounts used for acquiring, constructing or substantially rehabilitating the property. The regular tax is much more liberal.

The new law also gives a pardon of sorts to people who fall prey to the minimum tax and then go back to the regular tax in future years. The law provides a "minimum tax credit" that can be applied against regular tax in later years. The credit is intended to prevent double taxation of certain preferences, such as depreciation, that show up in a minimum tax calculation in the early years and again in the regular tax computation in later years. The credit doesn't apply to one-time exclusion, such as charitable contributions and tax-exempt interest.

21

AMERICANS LIVING AND GOING ABROAD

Americans working abroad will get a smaller exclusion from United States taxes under the new law. Beginning in 1987 they will be able to exclude only $70,000 of their foreign earnings each year from U.S. income taxes, down from $80,000 under the old law.

People earning more than $70,000, however, won't necessarily be hurt by the reduction. First, many companies have agreements with their employees under which the employer picks up the tab for any such tax increases. Second, the reduction in American tax rates could more than offset any additional tax resulting from the reduced exclusion.

Furthermore, the exclusion generally isn't of benefit to people working in foreign countries where taxes are high. American citizens, who are subject to U.S. taxes on their worldwide income, can claim a credit against their U.S. income tax liability for taxes paid to a foreign government on their foreign income. So if their foreign tax burden is higher than their U.S. tax liability, the credits normally take care of eliminating the U.S. tax on their foreign income. The exclusion isn't needed.

Thus, the reduced exclusion will primarily hurt Americans living in low-tax countries. They rely on the exclusion because foreign tax credits aren't sizable enough to wipe out their U.S. tax obligation.

NEW IRS FORM FOR PASSPORT APPLICANTS
When you apply for or renew a United States passport you will be given an extra new form to fill out. This one will not be from the State Department but from the Internal Revenue Service.

Although everyone applying for a passport will have to fill one out—even people taking a short vacation overseas—the new form is intended to help the IRS track down American citizens living abroad who fail to pay their share of United States income taxes either because they weren't aware they had a tax obligation to the United States or thought they could get away without paying. According to a recent congressional estimate, 61 percent of the 1.8 million American civilians living abroad fail to file a tax return.

American citizens who live abroad are required to file a federal tax return, since they are subject to tax on their worldwide income. Because of the $70,000 exclusion and the availability of foreign tax credits, Americans generally can partly or fully shield their foreign income from United States taxes. But some still end up owing taxes to the United States.

Foreigners applying for a permanent resident visa, known as a "green card," will also have to complete the new IRS form.

Congress hopes the new IRS form will prompt a lot of people living abroad to start filing returns. And if they aren't so prompted, then the IRS will at least have the information to contact the people who haven't been filing their returns. Failure to file the new information form can mean a $50 penalty.

RETIREES ABROAD SUBJECT TO WITHHOLDING

American retirees living abroad will find their pension benefits subject to new withholding rules. Beginning in 1987 the new law generally requires employers to withhold tax from pension payments sent to foreign addresses.

Under the old law, no tax was withheld from pensions unless the retiree requested it.

The reason for the change is that Congress suspected that a sizable number of Americans overseas who fail to file United States tax returns are retirees. And retirees are considered among the most likely to owe some tax because the $70,000 exclusion does not apply to pension income.

Even with the new information forms required of passport applicants, Congress felt compelled to take a bigger step with pensions. Tax writers were well aware that just because the IRS might be able to identify those who fail to file a tax return, collecting taxes from people in a foreign country is no easy task. So they decided to withhold tax on pensions before the money left American shores.

22

NEW FILING REQUIREMENTS AND PENALTIES

Estimated Tax Payments

If you are self-employed or a wage earner with outside income, you may have to make some larger estimated tax payments to the Internal Revenue Service under the new law in order to avoid penalties.

The new law requires that estimated tax payments, which have to be made in quarterly installments throughout the year, have to total at least 100 percent of the previous year's tax liability or 90 percent of the current year's expected tax liability. You can pay according to either formula, whichever is more beneficial for you. That 90-percent figure is increased from 80 percent under the old law. Amounts withheld from your wages count as estimated tax payments.

Congress decided to increase the minimum amount of estimated taxes to be paid through the year on grounds that all taxpayers should be as current in their tax payments as are the vast majority of wage earners who have taxes withheld from their regular paychecks.

WHAT ARE ESTIMATED TAX PAYMENTS?

Although everybody focuses on April 15 as the annual reckoning day for tax collection, the federal income tax is actually a pay-as-you-go system. You have to pay taxes as you earn the money or receive income during the year.

Most people do this through wage withholding at work. Employees have a certain amount of their income automatically withheld from their pay-checks by their employers who turn the money over to the Internal Revenue Service. Most people whose sole or primary source of income is wages do not have to make estimated tax payments.

But if you don't pay taxes through withholding or you don't pay enough tax that way, you may have to pay estimated tax. Estimated tax is the method you use to pay tax on income that is not subject to withholding, such as interest, dividends, alimony, prizes, stock market profits, and other capital gains. You may also have to pay estimated tax if you don't have enough with-held from your salary or pension income.

In any case, you do not have to make estimated tax payments if the tax to be paid by estimated tax payments is less than $500 for the year.

Congress thought that the old rules for estimated tax payments allowed many taxpayers to pay much less during the year than their ultimate tax lia-bility. By contrast, many workers subject to withholding have taxes with-held from their wages substantially in excess of their ultimate tax liability. That is why so many wage earners get a refund when they file their tax returns.

The change Congress made does not alter the rule of thumb as to which guideline to use in making estimated tax payments. If you figure your tax liability will be much higher than the previous year, you will pay less in estimated taxes during the year by basing the payments on 100 percent of the previous year's tax liability.

On the other hand, if you know your current year's liability will be less than or equal to the previous year's tax liability, you will pay less in esti-mated taxes by basing the payments on 90 percent of the current year's pro-jected tax liability.

The change from 80 percent to 90 percent becomes effective for pay-ments for the 1987 tax year. That means the estimated tax payment due Jan-uary 15, 1987—which is the final payment for tax year 1986—still falls under the 80 percent guideline.

The first quarterly payment to be affected by the 90-percent guideline will be April 15, 1987, which is the due date of the first payment for the 1987 tax year. Subsequent payments are due each year by June 15, Septem-ber 15, and finally January 15.

New Withholding Forms Needed

Every employee will be required to fill out a new W-4 wage withholding form with his or her employer by October 1, 1987. Because of the vast changes in the new law, the IRS was directed by Congress to revise the W-4 forms and also the withholding tables to take account of the changes.

The IRS planned to start shipping the new W-4s before the end of 1986, and you probably will be informed by your employer when the new forms arrive at work. Be aware that if you don't file a revised W-4 by October 1, 1987, your employer has to withhold income taxes from your paycheck as if you claimed only one allowance and checked "single" on your most recent W-4, or two allowances if you checked the "married" box on your last W-4. That may well be far short of the number of allowances you want to claim. The IRS is urging employees to fill out the new W-4s as soon as possible to ensure that the proper amount is withheld from their pay in 1987.

Reporting Tax-Exempt Interest on Returns

For the first time, all taxpayers will have to report all the tax-exempt interest they receive each year on their income tax returns. Even though most people will not have to pay a cent in taxes on this interest, Congress decided to make everybody declare it on their returns anyway.

Until now, only middle- and upper-income Social Security recipients whose benefits are partly subject to income tax have had to report tax-exempt interest on their returns. That reporting requirement went into effect on 1985 returns. For everyone else, no tax-exempt interest ever had to be reported. Because of this, more than a few husbands and wives who wanted to save some money on the side without their spouses knowing about it invested in tax-exempt bonds. Under the new law, such secrets will be hard to keep, particularly if a joint return is filed.

Congress wanted everybody to report tax-exempt interest partly to ensure compliance with the revised minimum tax, which will expose some people to tax on certain recently issued private-purpose tax-exempt bonds. Lawmakers also wanted to make sure that retirees correctly figure their tax, if any, on their Social Security benefits. That calculation requires adding tax-exempt interest to their other income.

Congress also thought that it would be helpful to have the information on tax-exempt interest on hand when it considers possible tax changes in the future. In recent years, tax writers have repeatedly debated the idea of making tax-exempt interest subject to tax in some way. The tax on Social Security benefits was the first encroachment. The new minimum tax represents the second.

The new reporting requirements are effective for the 1987 tax year, meaning most people will first have to report the interest in early 1988 when they file their 1987 tax year returns.

Tougher Penalties

The new law increases a variety of IRS penalties, making it more expensive for people who don't pay their taxes on time and for people who are careless, too aggressive, or outright dishonest in computing their taxes.

INTEREST PENALTIES

Interest on late tax payments and other underpayments gets more costly under the new law. After a four-year phase-out, you will no longer be able to deduct any of the interest. Furthermore, the interest you pay the IRS will be one percentage point higher than what the IRS has to pay you for overpayments. The rates were the same under the old law.

The interest rate on underpayments, which used to be pegged to the prime lending rate charged by banks, will now be set three points above the "federal short-term rate." This federal short-term rate will be based on the average market yield of outstanding government obligations of three years or less. The interest the IRS pays you for overpayments of tax will be set two percentage points above the federal short-term rate.

The IRS rates will be adjusted quarterly under the new law, rather than every six months, so that the rates better reflect prevailing market conditions.

To make underpayments an even more expensive proposition, the itemized deduction for interest on tax deficiencies is phased out under the new law, just as it is for other forms of personal interest. Only 65 percent of the interest is deductible in 1987, 40 percent in 1988, 20 percent in 1989 and 10 percent in 1990. After 1990, the deduction is completely gone.

The changes take effect beginning in 1987.

FAILURE TO PAY

If you fail to pay taxes when they are due, you can be subject to a penalty of one-half of 1 percent of the tax for the first month not paid. Subsequently the penalty increases by one-half of 1 percent for each month you don't pay. The penalty keeps increasing until it reaches the maximum 25 percent. Under the new law, the penalty increases to 1 percent, instead of ¹/₂ percent, once you have been notified that the IRS will levy upon your assets to collect past-due taxes. The IRS usually sends out four or five letters demanding payment before a levy is made. Congress decided to impose the additional penalty because the IRS has to use more expensive collection methods after the initial warnings.

SUBSTANTIAL UNDERSTATEMENT OF TAX

If you "substantially understate" your taxes on your tax return, the new law will impose a much harsher penalty. The penalty was increased from 10 to 20 percent by the new law. Congress subsequently passed budget legislation increasing it to 25 percent. The understatement is the difference between the correct tax and the tax shown on your return. You are deemed to have substantially understated your tax if your understatement is more than 10 percent of the correct tax or more than $5,000—whichever is greater. The amount of the understatement can be reduced if you have substantial authority for your position, such as court precedents, or you disclose on your return the relevant facts affecting the tax treatment of the item in question. The increase is effective for penalties assessed after October 21, 1986.

The increased penalty will make many tax advisers and taxpayers think twice before taking an aggressive position on the tax treatment of certain items on tax returns. "You've got to be very sure that you've got substantial authority for your position—particularly if the tax dollars are big," said Gerald Padwe, national director of tax practice at the accounting firm Touche Ross & Company.

TAX SHELTER PENALTIES

If you invest in a tax shelter that has a tax shelter identification number, you have to report that number on your tax return. If you fail to report the number under the new law you face a $250 penalty, up from $50 under the old law. The penalty applies unless failure to report the number is due to reasonable cause.

NEGLIGENCE PENALTY

The new law cracks down on people who fail to report on their tax return income that shows up on Form 1099 information reports that financial institutions and others are required to file with the IRS. Taxpayers also get copies of these reports. The new law presumes you are negligent and subject to penalty if you omit any income reported on any information return unless you can present "clear and convincing evidence to the contrary." The old law penalty used to apply only to interest and dividend information reports.

The negligence penalty, which is 5 percent of the full underpayment, is expanded to apply to all federal taxes. The old law confined the penalty to income, gift, and windfall profits taxes.

The changes apply to returns due beginning in 1987.

FRAUD PENALTY

The penalty for underpayment of tax due to fraud is increased from 50 percent to 75 percent. But the new law limits the penalty to that part of the penalty due to fraud, rather than the entire underpayment if any part was due to fraud. But once the IRS has established that fraud occurred, the taxpayer now bears the burden of proof to establish the portion of the underpayment that is not attributable to fraud. The provision applies to returns due beginning in 1987.

New Information Reports on Real Estate and Royalties

The new law also requires some new Form 1099 information reports to be made to the IRS. In recent years, Congress has sharply increased the types of transactions that have to be reported to the IRS so that the revenue service can use them as cross-checks to make sure that taxpayers are including the income on their tax return.

Beginning in 1987, real-estate transactions have to be reported to the IRS. The report generally has to be filed by the person responsible for the closing, which is usually the settlement attorney or the title insurance company. Otherwise the responsibility falls to the mortgage lender, the seller's broker, or the buyer's broker.

Persons who make royalty payments of $10 or more during the year to another person also have to file an information report. Under the old law, no report had to be filed unless the royalty payment totaled at least $600. Royalties include not only payments for rights to exploit oil and gas and other natural resources but also payments relating to copyrights, literary and musical compositions, artistic works, trade names, patents, etc.

Discouraging Tax Cheats?

When experts try to explain the motivating factors behind tax cheating and the underground economy, they often cite high tax rates and the public's perception that the tax system was unfair. Why should I pay my fair share of taxes if a lot of other people legally get away without paying theirs?

With tax rates sharply lowered and the system made much fairer—at least in the eyes of many tax reformers—will the new law discourage tax cheats and reduce the off-the-books, or underground, economy? Or will many people continue to evade paying their fair share?

Well, it is doubtful that millions of tax cheaters will suddenly start reporting all their income just because tax rates are lower and the system is perceived as fairer. But with rates lower, the incentive for evading taxes— and taking the risk of getting caught—will be reduced. And with the fairness question addressed, people will have one less excuse for violating the tax laws.

In addition, there are some provisions in the new law that will help taxpayers become more honest, including stiffer penalties. Retirees living abroad, who tend not to pay their fair share of United States taxes, will now have tax withheld on their pensions. Another provision will require parents to list the Social Security numbers of their children, a move aimed at preventing people from claiming extra exemptions for their dog, their cat, and fictitious dependents.

And with many deductions curtailed, taxpayers will have fewer opportunities for cheating. All of this will presumably allow the Internal Revenue Service to devote its resources to the tougher cases, such as people with cash businesses who have plenty of opportunity for underreporting income.

23

TRUSTS AND ESTATES

Trusts and Estates: An Overview

Like individuals, trusts and estates get new tax tables under the new law. The tables apply to non-grantor trusts, which are treated as separate taxable entities under both the old and new laws. The tables do not apply to Clifford Trusts, spousal remainder trusts, or other so-called "grantor" trusts. Grantor trusts are taxed directly to the grantor at his or her own tax rates.

TAX RATES FOR TRUSTS AND ESTATES

1987		1988	
TAXABLE INCOME	**RATE**	**TAXABLE INCOME**	**RATE**
0–$500	11%	0–$5,000	15%
$500–$4,700	15%	$5,000–$13,000	28%
$4,700–$7,550	28%	$13,000–$26,000*	33%*
$7,550–$15,150	35%	Over $26,000	28%
Over $15,150	38.5%		

NOTE: Tax tables apply to non-grantor trusts. Clifford Trusts, spousal-remainder trusts, and other so-called grantor trusts are taxed directly to the grantor of the trust.

* Taxable income between $13,000 and $26,000 is subject to a 5-percent surcharge reflecting the phase-out of the benefit of the 15-percent tax bracket. The surcharge effectively makes the top marginal rate on this income 33-percent.

Generation-Skipping Transfer Tax

The "Generation-Skipping Transfer Tax" was originally put into the law to catch people who tried to avoid paying estate taxes by passing their fortunes on to their grandchildren instead of their children. The new law is more lenient, but Congress felt the old law was so complicated that few taxpayers ever complied and the IRS had trouble enforcing it. The new law provides an exemption for transfers of up to $1 million for each donor. An additional $2 million exemption is given for each donee. Thus, a couple could pass on a total of $4 million to a grandchild without paying any generation-skipping tax. The extra $2 million exemption, however, expires on January 1, 1990, providing an incentive for people to make such transfers before then.

Generation-skipping transfers not covered by the exemptions are taxed at a 55 percent rate through 1987, and 50 percent thereafter.

ESTIMATED TAXES REQUIRED FOR TRUSTS AND ESTATES

Beginning in the 1987 tax year trusts and estates will be required to pay estimated tax, just as individuals have long been required to do. New estates, however, are not required to pay estimated taxes for their first two taxable years.

24

SECOND INCOMES AND SMALL BUSINESSES

Small Businesses

Many small businesses should make out well under the new tax law, particularly with the sharp drop in tax rates. Sole proprietors will benefit from the lower individual rates. And incorporated businesses will benefit from the reduced corporate rate, including the graduated rates available for small businesses. Self-employed individuals get a new deduction for a portion of their health insurance premiums. And small businesses get to write off up to $10,000 of their equipment purchases in the first year, double the amount of the old law.

Small businesses also were exempted from many of the harsher tax rule changes that will apply to larger companies. For example, small businesses with revenues of less than $5 million a year will still be able to use the cash method of accounting, which many small businesses find more advantageous than the accrual method. Under the cash method, businesses report income in the year when cash is received and deduct expenses when cash is paid out. This is the same method that individuals generally use in computing their personal taxes. Under the accrual method, income has to be reported when the goods are sold or services are rendered and expenses are deducted when obligations are incurred.

Small contractors with annual gross incomes of $10 million or less that complete contracts in less than two years can still use the completed contract method of accounting, which allows them to defer paying taxes on income until the project is completed. Larger contractors will be restricted in the use of the completed contract method.

But for many small businesses, the new tax law is a mixed bag. Businesses will lose the benefit of the investment tax credit. And depreciation write-offs for the purchase of equipment and machinery will not generally be as valuable as the old law provided. Retirement plan rules have been tightened, limiting the benefits allowed under tax-favored plans for owners of closely held businesses, and requiring greater coverage and benefits for employees.

CORPORATION VERSUS S CORPORATION

For the first time, individual tax rates will be lower than corporate rates under the new law. This historic change is bound to cause many small businesses that are incorporated to consider changing their legal structure to take advantage of the individual rates. Many tax professionals are advising their business clients to consider converting to "S corporation" status in order to take advantage of the lower individual rates.

With an S corporation, the corporation itself is not taxed. Rather, all the income, deductions, and credits are passed through to the shareholders of the business. An S corporation, which can have no more than thirty-five shareholders, also provides the limited liability advantage of a corporation.

Thus, the S corporation is being touted as a way to take advantage of the lower individual rates and avoid the much tougher corporate alternative minimum tax of the new law.

"The tax savings can be incredibly large over a period of time," said Theodore E. Stone, a senior manager at the accounting firm of Ernst & Whinney. "All businesses should be looking at it."

Switching to an S corporation may also be a way to avoid a double tax on the liquidation of corporations when they are sold. Under the new law, such gains will generally be taxed both at the corporate level and the shareholder level. This will raise the effective tax rate on corporate liquidations to 52.5 percent, from 20 percent under the old law when gains were generally taxed only at the shareholder level. Generally, liquidations completed before the end of 1986 are exempt from the new rules. Small closely held corporations valued at $5 million or less that are liquidated before 1989 are also exempt from the new rules. Partial relief is available to corporations valued between $5 million and $10 million.

There is also another reason to make a decision soon on whether to switch to S corporation status. Under the old law, if a business was sold within three years of the date on which the S conversion took effect, a

174

corporate-level tax was generally imposed. The new law generally extends this period to ten years, subjecting to the corporate-level tax any gains that arose before the conversion and which are recognized on the sale of the business. This change generally applies to S elections made after 1986. But smaller businesses are allowed relief from this provision if they elect S corporate status in time so that it is effective before 1989.

S corporations are not for everyone. Some people will find the additional tax-favored fringe benefits available to owners under the corporate status more than offset the advantages of switching to an S corporation. State and local tax laws can also reduce the appeal of S corporation status. In any event, whether or not to convert is something that you will need to sit down with your tax adviser to explore and to work out the calculations.

New Health-Insurance Deduction for the Self-Employed

Self-employed workers get a new tax deduction beginning in 1987 to help subsidize the cost of their health insurance. They get to deduct 25 percent of amounts paid for health-insurance coverage for themselves, their spouse, and their dependents.

Employees of corporations have long had the benefit of being able to fully exclude from taxes health insurance provided by their employer. While the 25-percent deduction available for self-employed workers still pales by comparison, Congress decided that it was time to narrow the gap between those who work for themselves and those who work under the corporate umbrella.

Besides the 25-percent limitation, there are a few other restrictions. The deduction cannot exceed net earnings from the self-employment business. Second, no deduction is allowed in any year that you are eligible to participate in a subsidized health plan of another employer or through your spouse's employer.

If you have employees, you generally will have to provide coverage for them as well to qualify for the new deduction.

The new law authorized the deduction only through 1989.

Writing Off a Car, a Computer, and Office Furniture

Cars, computers, office furniture, and other equipment used in your business will not be as heavily subsidized by the government under the new law.

You will no longer be able to claim the investment tax credit, which had been worth up to 10 percent of the cost of machinery and equipment. The credit was abolished retroactively to January 1, 1986. But you will still be able to write off the cost of business equipment over a period of years, even though the new law generally makes you do it at a somewhat slower pace. That means somewhat smaller deductions each year. Furthermore, the value of these deductions is reduced in value because of the lower tax rates. So you get less of a tax subsidy for making purchases. On the other side of the coin, the lower tax rates mean you get to keep more of the profits from your business.

The new depreciation schedules take effect for machinery and equipment placed in service beginning in 1987. If you placed it in service between August 1, 1986, and December 31, 1986, you have the option of using either the new or old depreciation system.

WRITING OFF UP TO $10,000 IN THE FIRST YEAR

Instead of depreciating the cost over a period of years, the new law gives you the option of writing off up to $10,000 in equipment the first year. That is up from $5,000 under the old law. The higher limit goes into effect beginning in 1987. This immediate write-off, known as "expensing," is limited to the amount of taxable income you have from the business. The higher limit should be especially helpful for small businesses. In fact, Congress limited it to small businesses. The $10,000 limit is reduced dollar for dollar where the cost of business equipment placed in service during the year exceeds $200,000.

DEPRECIATION WRITE-OFFS FOR CARS

If you use your own car for business, you have the option of figuring deductions by using the standard IRS mileage allowance (21 cents a mile for the first 15,000 miles of business use each year and 11 cents for each additional mile) or your actual operating expenses. Actual expenses, which include depreciation of the vehicle, will usually provide a larger deduction.

If you use your car more than 50 percent for business, you can write off the portion of the car's cost attributable to business on a five-year schedule, compared to three years under the old law. In reality, it will take you six years to write off the cost of the car under the new law because you only get a half year's worth of write-offs for the first year you put the car in service. So the rest spills over into a sixth year. As shown in the table, you would be able to write off 20 percent of the cost in the first year, compared to 25 percent under the old law. (If more than 40 percent of the year's equipment acquisitions were made during the last three months of the year, you may get even less than a half-year's worth of depreciation deductions. All property placed in service during any calendar quarter that year has to be treated as placed in service at the midpoint of the quarter.)

DEPRECIATION WRITE-OFFS FOR BUSINESS CARS

PERCENTAGE OF COST THAT CAN BE WRITTEN OFF EACH YEAR

YEAR	OLD LAW	NEW LAW
1	25%	20%
2	38%	32%
3	37%	19%
4	—	12%
5	—	12%
6	—	6%

YEARLY LIMIT ON DEPRECIATION DEDUCTIONS FOR CARS COSTING MORE THAN $12,800

YEAR	OLD LAW	NEW LAW
1	$3,200	$2,560
2	$4,800	$4,100
3	$4,800	$2,450
4	$4,800	$1,475
Subsequent years	$4,800	$1,475

SOURCE: Laventhol & Horwath

LUXURY CARS

If your car costs more than $12,800, the amount of deductions you can claim each year gets limited further. Congress imposed the same kind of limits under the old law because they didn't like the idea of having the federal government heavily subsidize the purchase of "luxury" automobiles. The new law trims back the annual limits even further to conform to the slower depreciation schedule, as the table makes clear. You will still be able to write off all the costs, but it will take you much longer to do so if the car costs more than $12,800.

WRITING OFF A COMPUTER

If you buy a computer that you use more than 50 percent of the time for business, you can write off the costs over six years, just as with cars. Under the old law, costs could be written off in five years. But as the table shows, the new law will let you write off 52 percent of the costs in the first two years compared to 37 percent under the old law. That is because the new law uses a formula that provides a bigger write-off upfront.

DEPRECIATION WRITE-OFFS FOR COMPUTERS

PERCENTAGE OF COST THAT CAN BE WRITTEN OFF EACH YEAR

YEAR	OLD LAW	NEW LAW
1	15%	20%
2	22%	32%
3	21%	19%
4	21%	12%
5	21%	12%
6	—	6%

SOURCE: Laventhol & Horwath

OFFICE FURNITURE

If you are writing off office furniture, the costs have to be spread over eight years, compared to five years under the old law. But in the first two years the new law allows you to write off a total of 39 percent of the cost, compared to 37 percent under the old law. As the table shows, deductions in the later years become much smaller under the new law.

DEPRECIATION WRITE-OFFS FOR OFFICE FURNITURE

PERCENTAGE OF COST THAT CAN BE WRITTEN OFF EACH YEAR

YEAR	OLD LAW	NEW LAW
1	15%	14%
2	22%	25%
3	21%	17%
4	21%	13%
5	21%	9%
6	—	9%
7	—	9%
8	—	4%

SOURCE: Laventhol & Horwath

USING YOUR CAR OR COMPUTER 50-PERCENT OR LESS FOR BUSINESS

If you use your car or computer 50 percent or less for business, you will have to settle for smaller deductions each year. First of all, you're not allowed to use the $10,000 "expensing" option.

Second, in the case of a car, eligible costs can be written off using the same timetable as cars used mostly for business. But you have to use a "straight-line" formula, under which deductions are more evenly divided over the period, rather than the "accelerated" method, under which you get bigger deductions in the early years.

In the case of computers, eligible costs have to be written off using the straight-line formula over a five-year period.

Deducting Your Home Office

Many people who claim deductions for a home office will unhappily discover that the new tax law puts tighter limits on these cherished write-offs.

For people who run businesses out of their homes, the home-office deduction vanishes into the woodwork if their business doesn't show a profit for the year. As for employees who have a legitimate excuse for writing off a home office, their deductions are scaled back as a result of the new limitations on "miscellaneous" itemized deductions.

SELF-EMPLOYED INDIVIDUALS AND PEOPLE WITH SIDELINE BUSINESSES

Under the old law self-employed individuals, including people with sideline businesses, were able to claim home-office deductions up to the amount of gross income generated by the business during the year. Beginning in 1987 the new law allows home-office deductions only to the extent of "net income"—which is gross income minus all other deductible expenses aside from the home office.

Assume, for example, you had a sideline business that generated $5,000 in gross income from the sale of dresses you made. Say you had $4,000 in deductible expenses, such as fabric, needles, thread, advertising, and so on. That gives you net income of $1,000, which is the maximum amount of home-office deductions you could claim. If, on the other hand, your deductible expenses exceeded the $5,000 in gross income, you would not be able to claim any deduction for your home office other than expenses, such as home-mortgage interest and property taxes, that are deductible without regard to business use.

Any home-office expenses that you are not able to claim in a given year are not forever lost. They can be carried forward and used in a future year—subject, of course, to the "net income" limitations. In other words, total home-office deductions in any year—including any carryforwards—are allowed only to the extent of net income from the business that year. For example, if you had $10,000 in gross income and $6,000 in deductible expenses other than the home office, you could claim up to $4,000 in home-office expenses. So if you incurred $3,000 in home-office expenses for the year, you could also claim up to $1,000 in home-office expenses that you could not claim in a previous year.

EMPLOYEES

Employees also get pinched under the new law for a number of reasons. They suffer because of the new 2-percent "floor" on miscellaneous itemized deductions and employee business expenses. In addition, the new law no longer allows home-office deductions when employees lease a portion of their home to their employer. Under the old law taxpayers were able to circumvent some of the home-office restrictions by using this lease arrangement.

QUALIFYING FOR HOME-OFFICE DEDUCTIONS

These new restrictions only add to the difficulty most people have in trying to write off a room or space they set aside in their home as a business office. Many more taxpayers aspire to claim deductions for a home office than actually qualify. If you do qualify, you may be able to claim deductions for depreciation, utilities, and other operating expenses attributable to that part of the house. Renters can deduct a proportionate amount of rent. But the guidelines are strict.

If you have a sideline business you may be able to qualify, but most employees have difficulty meeting the standards. Self-employed business people who work out of their home easily qualify, but for those with a shop or office elsewhere, qualifying will be more difficult.

There are several criteria. First, the space has to be used regularly and exclusively for business. The office does not have to be a separate room. It can be a corner of a studio or loft apartment, or even a dedicated space in a bedroom. But whatever area is designated as the home office, no other use can be made of the space.

The rules also require that the office be either the "principal place of business" or a place to "meet or deal" with customers or clients.

Employees have a tough time meeting the criteria because their principal place of business is usually considered their office at work. And they usually do not pass the second test of "meeting or dealing" with clients at home. Making phone calls from a home office has been interpreted by the courts to be insufficient for the "meeting or dealing" test. Even if one of the tests is met, employees still have another hurdle: Use of the home office must be for the convenience of the employer. Using a room to do paperwork brought home from the office—even if required by the employer—usually will not pass the other tests.

Someone who moonlights, such as a schoolteacher who runs a mail-order business from home as a sideline, can have a principal place of business for each job and thus qualify for the home-office deduction for the mail-order business. But a retail store owner who works at the store during the day and does paperwork at home at night would not likely be entitled to a home-office deduction because the shop would be considered the principal place of business.

A few taxpayers with two work locations have won some recent court victories. "In a few cases, the courts have permitted taxpayers to deduct an office at home when the predominant amount of their time is spent in their home office when compared to the other location," said Richard J. Stricof, a tax partner at the accounting firm of Seidman & Seidman. Some musicians with the Metropolitan Opera were allowed to claim home-office deductions after a federal appeals court agreed that their time and effort spent practicing at home exceeded their time performing at Lincoln Center. The same court sided with a college professor on grounds he spent 80 percent of his work time researching and writing at home and that his office at the university was not conducive to such scholarly endeavors.

Deducting Hobby Expenses

If you have income from a hobby, such as growing orchids or breeding dogs, you may have a tougher time deducting as many expenses related to your sideline venture than you did in the past. To deduct more under the new tax law, you will need to make sure your sideline activity is structured as a profit-motivated venture and not just a pleasurable diversion geared more for recreation than making money.

As in the past, if you have a sideline business—even if it is just a hobby— any income it generates is subject to tax, but you are also eligible to deduct expenses arising from the activity. How much you can deduct depends on whether the activity is primarily a hobby from which you do not expect to make a profit or an endeavor that you are seriously trying to make money at.

If the activity is a hobby, expenses are deductible only to the extent of the income generated during the year. If you sell $100 in orchids, for example, only $100 in expenses qualify for a deduction, even if you spent many times that amount on advertising, seeds, and the like. Furthermore, under the new law you may not even have a chance to deduct the $100. The reason is that hobby expenses can be claimed only as a "miscellaneous" itemized deduction, a category with much tougher restrictions under the new law. Beginning in the 1987 tax year miscellaneous itemized deductions will be lumped together with most employee business expenses, and the total will have to be reduced by 2 percent of your adjusted gross income. In other words, if your adjusted gross income is $50,000, the first $1,000 in miscellaneous and employee business expenses will not be deductible.

As a result of this new floor, you may have to resign yourself to the fact that you will no longer receive much, if any, tax benefit from your hobby. Just consider your hobby a pleasurable diversion and enjoy it. When you spend money on your hobby, simply keep in mind that the federal government will no longer help as much, if at all, in subsidizing the costs.

HOW TO AVOID THE HOBBY RESTRICTIONS

If your sideline business is more than just a hobby, you may be able to avoid the tight restrictions on hobby expenses. But you need to make sure that your business will pass muster with the IRS. Be prepared to demonstrate that you consider your sideline business a serious business venture geared toward making a profit. You can still enjoy what you do, but you also have to take steps that will convince the IRS that you are working hard to make your business profitable.

If you can do that, you will not be hampered by the 2-percent floor on miscellaneous deductions. Rather, you will be able to deduct expenses in full on the Schedule C tax form, where business income and expenses are reported. And you will be able to claim those deductions whether or not you itemize. In addition, you will be able to deduct more expenses than you generate in income from the business.

But to do all this, you will need to make sure that your sideline business measures up to IRS standards. This is especially important if you engage in an activity that is commonly regarded as a hobby, such as: raising horses; freelance writing, painting, or photography; growing trees or flowers; flying airplanes; chartering boats; racing cars; collecting antiques; or farming as a sideline business.

PROVING THAT YOU MEAN SERIOUS BUSINESS

Proving that your sideline business is more than a hobby will be somewhat tougher under the new law. Under the old law the IRS generally presumed the activity was profit-motivated if a profit was made in two out of five consecutive years. An exception was made for raising horses, which requires a profit in two out of seven years. The new law left the horse-raising test unchanged, but for other activities the presumption test will generally require a profit to be made in three out of five years, instead of two of five.

183

You can claim deductions during the test period. But if the IRS eventually rules that your business is a hobby, you can be assessed for back taxes for any excess deductions you claimed in the past.

If you don't meet the presumption test, you do not necessarily lose. The tax law recognizes that a variety of factors may prevent you from turning a profit in three out of five years even if you are working day and night to make the venture profitable. If, for instance, the presumption test was the final test of whether a business was a hobby, many full-time farmers would have been classified as hobbyists in the last few years. As a result, the IRS will look at other factors to determine whether your business is profit-motivated, such as whether your operation is being conducted in a businesslike manner, how much time and effort you spend at it, your expertise or the expertise of the advisers you consult, your success with previous ventures, and the earnings history of your venture.

Nevertheless, you should make every effort to meet the presumption test. One way to ensure a profit is to put off expenditures in years that the business does not generate much income. If you collect antiques, for example, you can easily show a profit by selling some of your holdings and waiting until a future year to acquire new pieces.

Be aware that even if you show a profit in three of five years, the IRS still can challenge your motives if your business seems less than a business. Say you raised orchids and sold a couple hundred dollars' worth a year, showed a small profit for three years, and then claimed $10,000 in expenses for the next two years. The IRS is likely to become suspicious of your intentions even though you technically met the presumption test. The tougher presumption test is effective beginning with the 1987 tax year.

25

CORPORATIONS

Overview of Business Changes

For corporate America, the new tax law provides hundreds of changes that will sharply increase the overall tax burden on business but also create a more level playing field for business. The tax code will no longer favor certain industries over others as heavily. In the process, the new system will create new winners and losers among industries as the corporate tax rate is sharply lowered and special industry tax breaks are curtailed.

Overall, business would pay about $120 billion more in taxes between 1987 and 1991 as a result of the corporate changes. But the increase will not be spread evenly across industries. Businesses that have long been favored with special tax benefits, such as manufacturers and military contractors, will see their tax burden rise under the new law. The reduction in the corporate tax rate will not offset the loss of those special breaks.

But the picture will be very different for many high-technology and service-oriented companies that have not been able to take advantage of special investment tax breaks in the past and have thus ended up paying close to the top 46-percent rate of the old law. They will see their tax bill fall substantially as the top tax rate drops to 34 percent.

To be sure, congressional tax writers lacked the political appetite to rid the tax code of all special industry breaks, so the playing field is still a bit bumpy. Most of the tax benefits for oil and gas drilling, for example, were retained; timber companies also retained many of their special breaks. But even where special breaks are retained, a vastly more potent minimum tax on corporations will sharply diminish the value of many preferences and ensure that every profitable corporation pays a minimum amount of taxes. The reduction in the corporate tax rate will also have the effect of diluting the value of any special tax breaks left in the code.

The new law makes fundamental changes in many long-standing tax benefits accorded particular industries. Large banks lose some of their most cherished tax benefits, including the deduction for bad-debt reserves and interest deductions on money borrowed to purchase tax-exempt bonds. Manufacturers will be hurt by the repeal of the investment tax credit. Cutbacks in depreciation write-offs are among a number of changes that will hit real estate hard.

Highlighted Corporate Changes

CORPORATE RATES

Corporate tax rates are reduced from 46 percent to 34 percent, with lower graduated rates for smaller businesses. The new rate structure is effective July 1, 1987. Income in taxable years that include July 1, 1987, but don't start on that date is subject to blended rates from the new and old laws. For instance, a corporation whose taxable year begins on January 1 will have a top rate of 40 percent for 1987.

CORPORATE TAX RATES

OLD CORPORATE TAX RATES FOR 1986		NEW CORPORATE TAX RATE TABLES [Effective July 1, 1987**]	
TAXABLE INCOME	RATE*	TAXABLE INCOME	RATE***
0–$25,000	15%	0–$50,000	15%
$25,001–$50,000	18%	$50,001–$75,000	25%
$50,001–$75,000	30%	Over $75,000	34%
$75,001–$100,000	40%		
Over $100,000	46%		

* A 5-percent surcharge is imposed on taxable income in excess of $1 million, so that the benefit of the graduated rates is fully eliminated when income reaches $1,405,000. Thus, a corporation with more than $1,405,000 pays a flat 46-percent tax.

** Because the new rate schedule is not effective until July 1, 1987, the rates for the 1987 tax year will be a blend of the new law rates and the old law rates in effect for 1986. Thus, the top corporate rate in 1987 will be 40 percent (blend of the 46 percent old law rate and the new law 34 percent rate) for a corporation whose taxable year starts on January 1.

*** The benefit of the graduated rates is phased out through the imposition of an additional 5-percent tax between $100,000 and $335,000 of taxable income. Thus, a company with more than $335,000 of income would pay tax at a flat rate of 34 percent.

INVESTMENT TAX CREDIT

The investment tax credit, worth up to 10 percent of the cost of purchasing machinery or equipment, was repealed retroactively to January 1, 1986. This will be the third time that the credit has been completely abolished since it was instituted during the Kennedy administration. It was revived each time, but the credit was conceived initially as being a temporary benefit. The repeal is expected to raise nearly $119 billion from 1987 to 1991, which by itself would more than pay for the corporate rate reduction.

CORPORATE CAPITAL GAINS

The preferential tax rate on corporate capital gains is eliminated for corporations, just as it is for individuals. Such gains will be taxed at regular corporate rates. Under the old law, the top rate was 28 percent. The change is effective beginning in 1987.

RESEARCH-AND-DEVELOPMENT CREDIT

The credit for increased research-and-development costs is extended through 1988 at a rate of 20 percent. Some of the rules relating to which costs qualify for the credit have also been tightened. Under the old law the credit was 25 percent and was scheduled to expire at the end of 1985.

CORPORATE MINIMUM TAX

To ensure that all corporations pay a minimum amount of tax, the new law includes a dramatically more potent minimum tax on corporations. The rate is set at 20 percent, up from 15 percent under the old law, and more tax preferences have to be added back to income in figuring the tax.

As a catchall, 50 percent of the excess of pretax "book income" over income calculated for minimum tax purposes is treated as a preference. Book income is the amount reported to shareholders on financial statements before deducting preferences. This will force companies to pay at least 10 percent of the profits they report to shareholders. This preference was included because of public criticism that some companies were reporting huge profits to their shareholders but ended up paying little or no tax. After 1989, book income is replaced with an "earnings and profits" formula, which is intended to raise about the same amount of money.

To prevent small businesses from having to cope with the alternative minimum tax, a $40,000 exemption is allowed. But the exemption is phased out at the rate of 25 cents for each dollar of income (as computed under the minimum tax) in excess of $150,000.

TARGETED JOBS TAX CREDIT

This credit, available to employers who hire economically disadvantaged or disabled workers, is extended for employees who begin work before 1989. It had been scheduled to expire at the end of 1985. The credit is 40 percent for the first $6,000 of first-year wages, down from 50 percent. No credit is available for second-year wages. The law also retains the 85-percent credit for the first $3,000 in wages paid to economically disadvantaged youths who are hired for the summer.

CORPORATE DIVIDENDS RECEIVED

The deduction for dividends that corporations receive is reduced to 80 percent, from 85 percent.

BUSINESS ENERGY CREDITS

Business energy credits, which were scheduled to expire at the end of 1985, are extended but reduced. Solar-energy credits are 15 percent in 1986, 12 percent in 1987, and 10 percent in 1988. Geothermal systems are 15 percent in 1986, and 10 percent in 1987 and 1988. Ocean thermal property is 15 percent through 1988. Biomass is 15 percent in 1986 and 10 percent in 1987.

FINANCIAL INSTITUTIONS

BAD DEBT RESERVES DEDUCTION: Large banks with assets of more than $500 million will no longer be able to claim a deduction for reserves they set aside to cover potential bad debts. No deduction will be allowed until actual loan losses occur and the debt is charged off on the institution's financial statements. The bad debt reserve deduction would be retained for smaller banks, thus leaving only about 450 of the nation's 13,500 banks affected by the repeal.

TAX-EXEMPT BONDS: Financial institutions would no longer be able to deduct interest on money borrowed to carry tax-exempt bonds. Under current law, they can deduct 80 percent of the interest. This change may have a significant impact on the municipal bond market, since financial institutions are major purchasers of tax-exempt securities.

MERGERS AND ACQUISITIONS

A number of provisions are intended to discourage corporate takeovers, or at least cause them to become more expensive to consummate.

GENERAL UTILITIES REPEAL: The favorable tax treatment accorded to corporate acquisitions under the so-called General Utilities doctrine, which arose from a 1935 Supreme Court ruling, is repealed. The doctrine provided a valuable exception to the general rule that profits from the sale of appreciated property are subject to double taxation; first to the corporation when the sale occurs, and then when the net proceeds are distributed to shareholders. The rule exempted tax at the corporate level. The new law will impose a tax at both the corporate and shareholder level, raising the effective tax rate on corporate liquidations from 20 percent to 52.5 percent.

GREENMAIL PAYMENTS: Corporations would not be able to deduct the cost of repurchasing its own stock from shareholders under "greenmail payments" to prevent a hostile takeover.

NET OPERATING LOSSES: Companies taking over money-losing corporations will be limited in the amount of the acquired corporation's losses they can use to reduce their tax bill. Some corporate takeovers have in the past been motivated by the ability to use these losses.

CASH METHOD OF ACCOUNTING
Corporations are generally prohibited from using this method of accounting for tax purposes and will be required to use the accrual method instead. Exempt from the provision are small businesses with gross income of $5 million or less and farming and timber businesses. Also exempt are personal service corporations engaged in the field of law, accounting, health, engineering, architecture, performing arts, consulting and actuarial science.

COMPLETED-CONTRACT METHOD OF ACCOUNTING
The new law limits the benefit of this method of accounting for long-term contracts, which allows military and general contractors to defer paying taxes on income until the project is completed. The provision affects contracts entered into after February 28, 1986. Exempt are contracts to be completed in two years or less by contractors with average gross incomes of $10 million a year or less.

NEW DEPRECIATION SCHEDULE

WRITE-OFF PERIOD	METHOD	TYPE OF ASSETS IN CLASS
3 years	200% declining balance	Racehorses; special tools in certain manufacturing; over-the-road tractors
5 years	200% declining balance	Computers and peripheral equipment; automobiles; typewriters; copiers; calculators; trucks; cattle; research and experimentation property; oil- and gas-drilling equipment
7 years	200% declining balance	Office furniture; commercial airplanes; single-purpose agricultural structures; various types of manufacturing machinery
10 years	200% declining balance	Ships
15 years	150% declining balance	Land improvements; billboards; telephone distribution plants
20 years	150% declining balance	Farm buildings
27.5 years	Straight-line	Residential buildings
31.5 years	Straight-line	Commercial real estate

BAD DEBT RESERVES

The new law eliminates the use of bad debt reserve deductions except for smaller financial institutions. Thus, bad debt deductions will be limited to actual loan losses.

TAXABLE YEARS OF PARTNERSHIPS, S CORPORATIONS, AND PERSONAL SERVICE CORPORATIONS

Partnerships, S corporations, and personal service corporations must generally adopt the same taxable year as that of their owners.

26

WHAT'S NEXT AFTER TAX REFORM?

When the new tax law was moving through Congress, many lawmakers hailed it as the tax bill to end all tax bills. The new law would bring to a halt the seemingly endless flurry of major tax changes that had marked the past decade. Americans would no longer have to live in a constant state of confusion and uncertainty over the tax environment.

Even before the ink on the tax bill was dry, there was already talk from many quarters about the next tax bill. Congressional tax writers acknowledged the likely need for a "technical corrections" bill in 1987 to fix mistakes made in the drafting of the new law. Technical corrections bills are common after a major piece of tax legislation is passed. Many tax lobbyists see a corrections bill as a potential opening for more substantive changes to be thrown in.

Even if the technical corrections bill remains largely technical in scope, many lawmakers expect there will be need for substantive tax changes in the years ahead.

If the economy weakens, some believe there might be pressure to bring back some of the investment incentives that were repealed—such as the investment tax credit—in an effort to stimulate the economy. The investment credit was reinstated twice before when the economy turned down. But now the climate is very different. Congress will find it tough to reinstate expensive tax benefits in the face of huge federal budget deficits.

HIGHER TAXES TO REDUCE THE DEFICIT?

In fact, Congress has been groping for ways to reduce the deficit to meet the terms of the Gramm-Rudman-Hollings balanced budget law. It is that search that many lawmakers believe will ultimately lead to future tax increases.

Representative Dan Rostenkowski, chairman of the House Ways and Means Committee, said the "fairest" way to raise more revenue would be to increase tax rates. Because of that possibility, congressional tax writers left intact the statutory structure of capital gains in the tax code to, in their words, "facilitate reinstatement of a capital gains rate differential if there is a future tax rate increase." Many members of Congress have already said they intend to strongly resist any attempt to raise tax rates. The Reagan administration is also strongly opposed to raising rates. "You don't need to worry about these rates being jacked up in this presidency," said Treasury Secretary James A. Baker 3rd.

Senator Bob Packwood, who will be replaced as chairman of the Senate Finance Committee by Lloyd Bentsen, a Texas Democrat, opposes the idea of raising rates, but suggested that revenues could be increased instead by curtailing more deductions and other tax preferences. But Congress may well find it difficult to raise substantial amounts of new revenue by trying to scale back more tax benefits. Congress went far in that direction in the new tax law, and many tax writers believe they have gone about as far as political limits allow. President Reagan has repeatedly stated his opposition to any increase in taxes.

To pick up added revenues, Congress is likely to at least consider raising excise taxes—such as those on gasoline, cigarettes, and alcohol—as an alternative to income tax changes. If very large amounts of revenue are needed, some tax experts believe Congress will be forced to consider some new form of consumption tax, such as a national sales tax or a European-style value-added tax.

Many people in the business community strongly support a consumption tax as a way to avoid being hit themselves with higher taxes on their profits. But proponents face an uphill battle generating support among lawmakers. Democrats generally oppose value-added taxes—which are levied on businesses at each stage of production and thereby are built into the price of goods—on the ground that they hit lower- and middle-income individuals hardest; they tend to spend a large proportion of their income on consumption.

Many Republicans, while opposed to increases in income tax rates, also oppose consumption taxes on the ground that they can be powerful revenue sources and thus make it difficult to restrain federal spending.

Nevertheless, some lawmakers have been seriously discussing the idea of a consumption tax as a way out of the deficit bind.

LIFE UNDER THE NEW LAW

In the interim, the Internal Revenue Service has the monumental task of implementing the new law, redesigning tax return forms, and drawing up regulations to give taxpayers detailed guidance on the new provisions. At the same time, taxpayers will have to adjust their financial lives to the new law.

Whether real or imagined, much of what happens in the American economy over the next few years is likely to be attributed to the new tax law—particularly if there are problems. Norman Ornstein, a congressional expert and a senior fellow at the American Enterprise Institute, expects that companies will blame any earnings decline they suffer on the new tax law, whether it's the real culprit or not. At the very least, he said, it's a convenient excuse and much better than executives blaming themselves for the poor performance. If college tuition bills go up, do not be surprised if the college president encloses a letter with the bill blaming the increase on the new tax law. Every future rent increase may well be accompanied by a note from the landlord blaming the new tax law for the need to raise rents.

Certainly many adjustments are bound to occur. But the basic fabric of American life is not likely to be radically altered by the new law. People will still get married and divorced, have children, go to college, buy homes, take vacations, and go out to nice restaurants. Taxes don't play that central a role in life's most important decisions. Nor should they. In fact, that is what the new tax law is largely about: further reducing the influence of taxes in your life. Allowing you to keep more of every extra dollar you earn and giving you greater freedom to do with it what you like—instead of the government telling you the preferred channel.

CALENDAR OF EFFECTIVE DATES OF MAJOR PROVISIONS

This calendar shows when major provisions are generally effective. Be aware that some provisions include special transition rules and exceptions for certain classes of taxpayers.

JANUARY 1, 1986

Investment tax credit is repealed.

MARCH 1, 1986

Clifford Trusts created after this date, as well as additional amounts placed in previously existing trusts, are subject to new rules that will tax earnings at the grantor's tax rate rather than the child's.

JULY 1, 1986

Federal workers whose retirement is effective after this date lose benefit of three-year tax-free period for pension payouts.

AUGUST 8, 1986

Certain private-purpose tax-exempt bonds issued henceforth become subject to new alternative minimum tax, beginning in 1987.

AUGUST 17, 1986

• Scholarship or fellowships granted henceforth are subject to new restrictions that may make them partially taxable.

• Mortgage interest debt incurred henceforth is subject to new restrictions. Deductions limited to original purchase price of the home plus improvements and amounts borrowed against the home for medical or educational expenses.

OCTOBER 22, 1986

• President Reagan signs the Tax Reform Act of 1986 and enacts the legislation into law.

• Tax shelters invested in henceforth generally do not qualify for transition relief for deductibility of tax losses.

JANUARY 1, 1987

• Top individual tax rate drops to 38.5 percent and a five-bracket tax system goes into place for one year before the new two-bracket system is put in place in 1988.

• Personal exemption increased to $1,900.

- Standard deduction increased slightly, except for elderly and blind taxpayers, who receive fully phased-in amount.
- Earned income credit increased.
- Numerous tax benefits are eliminated, including the charitable deduction for non-itemizers; the state and local sales tax deduction; adoption expense; two-earner deduction; income averaging; political contributions credit; and the limited exclusions for unemployment compensation and dividends.
- Numerous tax benefits are scaled back, including the medical expense deduction, employee business expenses, business meal and entertainment expenses, investment interest, moving expenses, and foreign earned income exclusion. Mortgage interest deduction faces new restrictions.
- The new individual and corporate alternative minimum tax provisions take effect.
- Various IRS penalties are increased.
- Only 65 percent of tax shelter losses and consumer interest expenses are deductible under phase-out transition rule.
- Long-term capital gains exclusion is eliminated. Top rate for long-term gains is capped at 28 percent, while top rate on short-term gains is 38.5 percent.
- Changes in tax treatment of younger children's savings accounts take effect.
- Business property placed in service henceforth subject to new depreciation rules.
- Self-employed individuals get new deduction for 25 percent of health insurance premiums.
- Various changes in retirement plans take effect. Individual Retirement Account deduction restricted for certain middle- and upper-income taxpayers covered by an employer pension plan. Maximum contribution limits to 401(k) plan and various other retirement plans are reduced.

APRIL 15, 1987

Due date for 1986 tax returns and last opportunity for some people to take a deduction for Individual Retirement Account contributions.

JULY 1, 1987

Corporate tax rates are reduced to 34 percent, from 46 percent.

SEPTEMBER 30, 1987

Deadline for filing revised Form W-4 with your employer.

DECEMBER 31, 1987

Tax exclusions for company-sponsored educational assistance plans and group legal services plans are scheduled to expire.

JANUARY 1, 1988

- Individual tax rates lowered to 15 and 28 percent.
- Parents filing tax returns due henceforth are required to include the social security number of any dependent at least five years old who is claimed as an exemption.
- Standard deduction fully increased for all taxpayers.
- Personal exemption increased to $1,950.
- Distinction between long-term and short-term capital gains disappears. Capital gains are taxed at

regular rates of 15 and 28 percent (33 percent for certain upper-income taxpayers).

• 40 percent of tax shelter losses and consumer interest expense allowed as a deduction.

DECEMBER 31, 1988

Research and development credit scheduled to expire.

JANUARY 1, 1989

• Quicker vesting requirements for employee pension plans take effect.
• Personal exemption increased to $2,000.
• Tax rate schedules and standard deduction start being adjusted for inflation each year.
• 20 percent of tax shelter losses and consumer interest still allowed as a deduction.

DECEMBER 31, 1989

Self-employee health insurance deduction scheduled to expire.

JANUARY 1, 1990

• 10 percent of tax shelter losses and consumer interest still allowed as a deduction.
• Personal exemption starts being adjusted for inflation each year.

JANUARY 1, 1991

Deductions for tax shelter losses and consumer interest are completely phased out.